# Barb's Journey

## A Story of Faith, Family, Friends and Perseverance

BARBARA PRAY

ISBN-13:
978-1499789348

# DEDICATION

I would like to dedicate this book to my husband, Jim. I love my husband more than words can say and am thankful that he didn't leave me when I needed him the most. He was there every second of every day holding my throw up pails and holding me all night. I know from seeing it myself, people that had somebody there with them did better than those who were alone. It made my days shorter when we prayed together, played games together and talked about our family.

Jim would always console me and make me feel better. He would walk a mile just to get me a hamburger that I could not eat because the smell would make me sick. I know that most husbands would leave from dealing with it for 30 years. That is why I love my husband so very much.

ACKNOWLEDGMENTS

I would like to express my gratitude to the many people who helped me write this book. It took a lot of time. It was very stressful recalling the big "C" moments in my life.

I would like to thank Rosemary Gold for giving me the support that I needed to help me write this book. Thank you to Nicole Olson for the main editing on the book. Thank you to Kari Hewitt for pushing the book to get it done, for organizing, typing, editing the pictures for the cover and the editing on the book. Thank you to Author Jeremy Hone for scanning the pictures for the book. Thank you to Kayla Suther for taking pictures for the cover. Thank you to Author Kathleen Aadland Wojcik for editing and technical assistance in publishing.

Thank you to my three children, Kelly Pray, Paula Winther and Michelle Kelly for writing their feelings about what they were going through at that time. A special thank you to my grandchildren, Alexa, Madeline and Christopher for there letters to me.

Barb

**Romans 5:2-5 THROUGH HIM WE HAVE ALSO OBTAINED ACCESS BY FAITH INTO THIS GRACE IN WHICH WE STAND, AND WE REJOICE IN HOPE OF THE GLORY OF GOD. NOT ONLY THAT, BUT WE REJOICE IN OUR SUFFERINGS, KNOWING THAT SUFFERING PRODUCES ENDURANCE, AND ENDURANCE PRODUCES CHARACTER, AND CHARACTER PRODUCES HOPE, AND HOPE DOES NOT PUT US TO SHAME, BECAUSE GOD'S LOVE HAS BEEN POURED INTO OUR HEARTS THROUGH THE HOLY SPIRIT WHO HAS BEEN GIVEN TO US.**

# PREFACE

## Cinco de Mayo

**"...Be not afraid, only believe" (Mark 5:36, KJV)."**

Most of our lives operate on calendars. We schedule appointments, meetings, birthday parties, and any number of other activities. Most of those dates are innocuous and mean very little past the actual event. But there are lots of other dates that are memorable and bring us back to something special or important. With each passing year, we pause, if only for a moment, and recall the importance of the date and the significance it had on our lives.

Like all of you, I have so very many days that I celebrate. My wedding, the births of my children and grandchildren, great accomplishments and major life changes make the list. But the one date that truly has shaped my life in ways I would never wish on anyone, is Cinco de Mayo. Before 1984, the fifth of May was an insignificant day in my life. Cinco de Mayo, the celebration of freedom in Mexico, is probably an important reminder to all who understand its premise and have an allegiance to the country that celebrates, similar to that of Independence Day in the United States, but for me, it wasn't terribly important. It was just another day.

Some might say that the significance of Cinco de Mayo provided me with my own freedom, and I guess that could seem plausible, but at the time it felt like more of a death sentence. In so many ways, I truly was desperately searching for my own freedom – freedom from pain, freedom from feeling like a hypochondriac, freedom of knowing that I was right and something was happening within my body. And on May 5, 1984, I was finally given the information I needed to understand the rebellion that was taking place within me. I won't go as far as to say that I found my own freedom, because that date just as aptly signifies my own hell, but it did provide me with the path that has guided me through my whole life. Cinco de Mayo (May 5$^{th}$) in 1984 was the day I was diagnosed with cancer.

The official diagnosis was non-Hodgkin's Lymphoma in the fourth stage of development as well as cancer of the liver, bone marrow, stomach and spine. In 1984, fourth stage of cancer meant certain death. It was almost always translated into a percentage of chance for cure and approximate time left before death. In my case, I was given a less than 10 percent chance to live and a guesstimate of approximately 1-2 months to live.

Obviously, I did not die.

I'm not sure why I was spared. Many would say that I was one of the "lucky" ones, but I didn't really feel lucky. I was most certainly a statistical anomaly. Over the years, I have had many instances where I have felt a greater understanding of my life's purpose, but I don't really know that it is an answer to the question. Maybe throughout the process of writing my story I will be provided a self-awareness that I have yet to achieve. And maybe I won't.

During my initial treatment, I met many other cancer patients who were being treated at the University of Minnesota Hospital at the same time that I was, and sadly, most that were diagnosed as stage four died. In fact, all but one of my fellow cancer-fighters died prior to me even leaving the hospital.

The initial diagnosis was more than overwhelming and took me a long time to accept. At diagnosis, I was so very fearful of death. I am sure some of it was fear for myself, but I remember feeling a strong fear for my children. I was the mother of three children, and they needed their mother. I needed them. I fought to survive for them. In my darkest hours, I thought about my children and prayed that God would give me the strength to make it through that day so that I might live another.

Even today, I think about death all the time. The fear I once had has changed to acceptance. I don't want to die, but I know there is a better life waiting for me. I have been given the gift of seeing my children grow into adulthood. I have had the great pleasure of welcoming grandchildren. I still fight for my own survival, but it is a different kind of fight now than it was when I was a young mother. I am in a place now where I feel that if it is my time to go, I will be ready. But I will keep fighting until that day arrives.

For the past several years, I have had so many people tell me, "Barb, you need to write a book and share with others why you are still alive." That is such an interesting comment, too, I think, because I don't really know why I'm still alive. I know that there were so many days when I was in such pain that I wished for death rather than continue through the pain, but I made it through. My friends, family, and faith helped me survive the toughest times.

Mine is a story of survival, most definitely. I'm not sure why my life was spared, and I'm not sure I can shed light on the subject of why I am alive. But I will write my story and share it. This book is not for those with cancer, though, either currently fighting or in remission. My story is for everyone else. I write it for those who will never understand how difficult it is to be called "a cancer survivor."

My name is Barb Pray, and I have been surviving cancer for 30 years. People refer to me as "a cancer survivor", but every day I continue to fight the battle. The cancer is gone from my body, but it can never be a memory. It left me a paraplegic, caused overwhelming depression and continued pain.

I have endured over 40 surgeries, a multitude of treatments, and piles of bills. The cancer itself is gone, and I am a changed person because of it. I am strong. I am a survivor. I say this as a fact, because I've earned it.

My life has been hard for as long as I can remember. Very little about my story is easy to share. I cry often, when remembering the past, but I try to convince myself that I wouldn't have wanted to miss this day. And most of the time, I believe it. I hope and pray that telling my story can provide insight into what surviving cancer means. I hope that my story inspires you. And I thank you Lord for allowing me to tell my story…

## THROUGH THE GEORGETOWN YEARS

I think back to our early lives and the time and all of the decisions made by the young Jim and Barb and how they shaped our lives. About midway through his senior year, Jim decided to quit school. At that time, he was convinced that he needed to work on his dad's farm. He also had been suspended from school for two weeks for playing hooky. Of course, he felt that the punishment was unfair even though he really was skipping school to see me. He was caught red handed when one of the teachers at my school, approximately 20 minutes from his, saw him driving around our school waiting for me. My teacher called his principal and he was suspended. One of the hazards of living in a small town is that everyone knows everyone else's business.

So many young couples can relate to the struggle of the early years being married. My husband, Jim, and I were no different. Boy, did we struggle those first few years. We married very young, and I am not always sure we would have plunged into marriage if not for the unexpected pregnancy that gave us our oldest child, Kelly. In addition, we had no classroom education past high school, and although we were both hard-working, finding a decent paying job was pretty tough, given our position. We struggled to make ends meet our first five years of marriage. It still shocks me to think that we often made less than $100 dollars a month.

Regardless we kept trying. I worked as a waitress at the local cafe, and Jim did the best he could to provide for our growing family. Jim was a good kid who turned into a great man. He is an honest, hard-working farmer who never shied away from hard work and if given a job to do, he would do his best to do it well. But in those early years, it felt like he moved from job-to-job to make just a little more money than the last.

Jim learned of a general manager opening for a large grain elevator in Georgetown, Minnesota, and although he was pretty certain that he wasn't qualified for the position because he had no experience working in such a big elevator, he was too young, and he didn't have the appropriate education, he applied anyway. To our surprise, the company wanted to interview him for the position.

Of course, we were beyond excited and trying very hard not to get our hopes up too high. I went with him to the interview, and we dreamed about the great opportunity and for the inevitable increase in salary. I remember him joking with me that whatever they offer him would not be enough, and he was going to ask for more. I laughed and thought it was pretty funny. We were both working and barely making ends meet, and he started talking about turning down a job that he had not yet been offered. That intimate moment stands out so vividly in my mind, even today.

He went into the interview and I anxiously waited for him. He came out of the interview and was so excited because he had been offered the job and it came with a great salary and a house for us to live! And not only that, he did exactly what we had talked about in the car a few hours earlier. He told them he needed more! He proceeded to negotiate for more money and asked that the carpet be replaced in the house. They agreed! I could hardly believe it. I was so proud of Jim and excited to move into what we were certain was right for us and that we had finally made it.

When Jim accepted the general manager position at the grain elevator in Georgetown, Minnesota, he was 26-years-old. Although he had a good understanding of the business, he did not have a lot of experience, nor did he have the educational qualifications for a managerial position. I am still convinced that they saw what I did when I looked at my husband. He was a confident, hardworking man with great capabilities.

Moving to Georgetown was a dream come true for Jim and I. At that time in our marriage, we had three young children, our son, Kelly, (8) and our daughters, Paula (7), and Michelle (4). We had the same dream for our kids that most parents do and wanted their lives to be easier than we remember ours to be. With Jim's new position, I would be able to give up my job as a waitress to stay home and care for our young family. I remember talking and dreaming all the way back to our hometown of Putney, South Dakota. I had visions of making a home for our family and spending time with the children. Jim told me that he would buy me a new wedding ring with a diamond.

We were all so young. And happy. It was the happiest time in my life and at that time I felt nothing could change this. The three years we lived in Georgetown were reminiscent of my own childhood. I grew up in a small town with one brother, the oldest, and three sisters, me the third of four girls. My father, Marvin, was the owner of a grain elevator and my mother, Mae, stayed home to take care of all of us kids.

Although there were many things I loved about my childhood and hoped to recreate for my own children, I wanted to be a more hands-on mother than my own was. Although Mom was home all day, she never spent a lot of time with us. She was good to us and we knew she loved us all, but she never really talked to us. I can't remember her helping me with homework or even going to any of my school functions. I did not want to do the same with our children. It was important to Jim and me to spend time with our children and be a part of their school functions, and Jim's new job made it possible for me to do this.

It was also very important to Jim and I that we spend time together as a family every single day. As a result, we never missed a dinner together. Each weekend, we would make the kids' favorite meal, homemade chicken noodle soup. After church the kids and I would roll out the dough, boil our own noodles, and eat as many as we added to the soup. I have to admit that this was my favorite meal as well. I do love homemade chicken noodle soup and the time with my kids each Sunday was such a special time for us.

As I've gotten older and raised my children, I often think about my own childhood. Although I wanted to be involved in all aspects of my kid's lives, and I would've loved to have had more time playing with my mom, I now understand that their view on life was very different, probably because of the time period that they grew up in. Both my parents lived through the early 30s and their lives were hard. The priorities in our home were set for work. My father worked at his grain elevator, my mom helped with the accounting for the elevator, and my brother, sisters, and I were responsible for chores as well. I was always given the outdoor chores, which suited me well. With my own children, I wanted to find a balance between instilling the importance of being a hardworking individual with the fun parts of childhood. I hope that I succeeded in that.

The small community of Georgetown had a total population of approximately 100, and was surrounded by family farms. My whole family felt immediately accepted into the community, and we made many friends in the time we lived there. In fact, I met one of my very best friends, LaDonna there. She was 20 years older, but we both had this crazy connection that can't be explained. LaDonna turned out later to be such a vital supporter for me during my battle with cancer. She was always there to talk with and help me work through my most difficult times of my life.

We worked easily into a routine once we were settled into our new home. Kelly and Paula attended the elementary school, which was about two blocks from our house. Jim went to work, and Michelle and I had our own little routine. We started each day getting the others off to work and school, and then we would share a breakfast of toast and cheese. Michelle laughs now, because we never changed our menu, but I notice that she still likes to have toast and cheese, especially with her own daughter. Passing on our breakfast ritual makes me smile.

After breakfast, we would play a workout record and exercise. We learned the exercises by looking at the pictures on the album cover, similar to a Jane Fonda workout tape, but without the video. After we exercised, we would clean the house, make lunch for Jim, and then have the afternoon to ourselves. In the afternoons, we would visit friends, go shopping, or do something together.

Spring and fall were the busiest times of the year for Jim. He often worked 12-14 hours, six to seven days per week during the busiest times. Although we missed him, we knew that this job was what gave us the opportunity to provide the life for our kids we wanted. During the winter months, Jim spent a lot more time with all of us and we treasured those times.

Although Jim is typically a home body, he occasionally spent time at one of the local pubs visiting with the local farmers. Jim recognized the importance of taking time to see his customers in the community, even though that portion of his job was always the most difficult for him. Kelly often liked to visit Jim at the elevator or at the local pub. He quickly learned, and kept it a secret from his sisters, that Jim was often easily persuaded into giving him extra treats. Trips to the elevator and the pub often meant soda, snacks, and money for pinball.

The girls were more inclined to spend time with me at home. Paula, especially, was quiet and shy like her dad, and she loved to clean. She would clean everything in the house until it was spotless. She and Kelly had a deal that he watched over her, and she cleaned his room for him.

Michelle, the youngest, always stuck close to home and mom. She spent hours by herself in her room playing with Barbie dolls. She accumulated quite a collection of Barbie dolls, doll houses and other Barbie accessories. Jim's mother, Meta, did a lot of knitting and crocheting, and every time she would visit she would get a new order of clothing for Barbie dolls. Her Barbie clothes took up a whole suitcase all by themselves. I remember Michelle playing with her dolls and giving them orders as I might give to her and her siblings, and then she would give the orders to her brother and sister and occasionally to Jim and me. At a very young age, she seemed to have and share her many opinions.

Having grown up on a farm and loving the lifestyle, Jim made a name for himself in the elevator business and seemed to really have a good relationship with the local farmers. He always wanted to be a farmer, but with the promotion as manager, and the great salary, we didn't consider farming as an option for making a decent living. Besides that, I loved our new life and the kids were happy too. I thought that we would stay in Georgetown forever.

The job itself was one that was perfect for Jim in many ways. He had never shied away from the physical labor and worked hard. Jim is a very quiet man, but was easily able to communicate with others. He wasn't someone who flew off the handle, but always made it clear to others where he stood. The continued frustration he felt in his job was one that was troublesome to both of us, but we never really discussed a change. In fact, if asked at that time, I was dead set against any change because Georgetown was our home.

But, as with everything, life changes. The pressure on Jim at work continued to build. The larger farmers, members of the board, were pushing the elevator to make changes that were great for them, but not for the smaller farmers. Jim often felt torn and was forced to accommodate the larger farmers, and struggled with it. Then, Jim received a call from his dad asking him to come home and work the family farm. Jim had always wanted to take over the family farm, but I was devastated.

At the time, I could not understand, but it seemed that Jim had his mind made up. It was almost as if he knew we needed to go back. I begged and pleaded with Jim not to move us back to a town we were so excited and thankful to move away from just a few years earlier. But his mind was made up and we were moving. Now, I see that without this move I would never have made it through my cancer.

## FAMILY FARM

The move to Groton to Jim's family farm was one of sorrow. We were so sad to be leaving a home we loved and the friends we had made. Additionally, the move brought us into a living situation that was less than ideal. Our family of five was forced to move into a small, probably around 900 square feet, two bedroom home. Jim and I had one bedroom and the girls shared the other. Kelly was moved into the front porch that was turned into a makeshift bedroom, barely big enough to fit a twin bed and small dresser. The front porch was definitely not meant to be a bedroom. It was surrounded by windows and had no direct heat.

In my logical mind, I knew that this living arrangement was temporary. We would only live in that house for about a year while we were planning a home to be put out onto the farm, one that eventually became our home for the next 25 years. However, the move into the tiny house paired with the fact that I was so sad and the kids were crying at night because they missed their friends was a difficult transition for all of us. I just did not know if we would ever be happy with this decision to move back to the family farm. Nothing about it made sense to me. The question of why we made this move was always on the forefront of my mind.

On top of the stress of moving, I knew I would have to go back to work. Jim used the money we had saved while living in Georgetown to buy milking cows and to build the new house on the farm. We did save a fair amount of money, but not nearly as much as we would've liked to because we only had three years to do it and were raising three kids at the same time. The house was actually a double wide trailer and we put a basement underneath, but it was a decent sized home and it cost much less than building.

As with everything in life, time helped all of us to adapt to our new surroundings. We began to accept our new, old town, and the kids made friends. I don't remember this time as one of happiness, but it was a situation that I gradually accepted. Looking back, I realize that this may have been God's way of setting my family and me up for the future. All of the pieces were being put together so that when the cancer struck me, we

were in the place where we had the support and care that we needed.
My first hint of health troubles came in 1982 when I fell hard on the ice and hit my tailbone. It hurt like the dickens, but I was sure it would get better with time. I didn't have the time to sit around and heal as I probably should have, because I needed to work. Plus, we literally lived from paycheck to paycheck, so missing work was not an option. But days of pain in my lower back turned into weeks and months. I continued to work and complained until Jim told me to see the doctor. I saw the doctor and he prescribed some pain pills and muscle relaxants. Although that helped, I had a nagging feeling that something else was wrong.

I tried to convince the doctor to look a little deeper, and eventually was referred to a specialist. After seeing the back specialist, surgery was suggested. The doctor felt that I had injured a disc in my back when I fell and hadn't given it enough time to heal. The surgery was supposed to be simple and I was assured that I would be good as new by the time school started. So, I had the surgery.

In December of that same year, I began suffering from upper back pain. It was like needles pricking between my shoulder blades. Once again, I didn't want to take time out of our lives to rest and recover, so I kept moving. Jim and I planned a California vacation and took the kids on the trip for their Christmas vacation. We had such a wonderful time! We visited Knott's Berry Farm, Disneyland and saw the Rose Parade. It was a vacation of a lifetime! We made such treasured memories on that trip.

The needle pricking pain in my back had become almost continuous by then, but I decided that I could live with it. It was not as severe as the lower back pain, and I kept reminding myself that I had a checkup in March with the doctor who had done my previous back surgery. At that appointment, I mentioned the upper back pain, but the doctor just brushed it off. He went so far as to tell me that my back was fine and indicated that the problem could possibly be in my head. He said it using a professional terminology, but I got the gist.

My friend, Julie, had gone with me to the appointment and we visited about how the doctor had treated me. We were still talking about the appointment when we stopped to see my parents on the ride home. I tried to visit as much as possible, and had brought my dad some cookies on this trip. I remember sitting in my parent's living room and visiting about the appointment and life with the kids, and then waking up a bit later with my parents worrying. They asked if I was sleeping, how I was feeling, and how long these symptoms had been causing me pain.

Parents have a way of getting us to break down and tell the truth, so I unloaded the story of my chronic back pain and how I hadn't been sleeping well for a long time. I explained that getting comfortable never seemed possible when I did try to sleep. My dad insisted that we take the recliner in his living room home with us because I had been able to sleep in the chair, and he wanted me to rest and feel better.

When getting ready to leave for home, recliner all loaded up into the vehicle, Julie asked Mom if Dad was sick. She noticed that he looked tired and pale. Mom said that she'd noticed he had been sleeping more and seemed always to sweat. Although I was concerned about Dad, I didn't think much about it on the ride home because as we were driving along, a deer jumped right out in front of us and flew right over the front bumper of the car. Neither was hurt, thank goodness, and we were so late getting home. Little did I know that our concerns about my dad's health was much more concerning than we thought.

Jim was relieved when I got home safely. We talked about the exciting day, Julie's suspicions regarding Dad's health, the newly acquired recliner, and finally Jim inquired about the doctor appointment. I told him the story of the doctor and his cruel bedside manner. I was still upset about the appointment and ruminating about the blistering words that the pain was "in my head." In his usual, practical way, Jim simply made the decision to find a new doctor.

The new recliner was a godsend. I was still having constant pain, but was able to find relief and sleep through the night in the recliner. And, as it always does, life continued to move quickly. The main event in the next months was preparing for Kelly's upcoming confirmation. I was so proud of him for completing the classes and taking this big step, and a little back pain wasn't going to stop the celebration.

I planned the celebration and invited family to come share the day with Kelly My parents attended, and once again, my dad didn't look well. He didn't even eat any cookies, which was strange for him. They even left early because Dad was so tired. An eerie, uncomfortable feeling crept over me and it seemed to fill my entire being. I couldn't put my finger on it, but I couldn't shake my concern. Mom called later that evening and shared that she planned to take Dad to the doctor as soon as she could make an appointment.

The doctor appointment revealed that Dad was suffering from lung cancer. We were devastated! A referral to Rochester, MN, was made and Dad was scheduled to have surgery to remove the tumor. My sister, Madonna, and Mom were both going to Rochester, but I felt it necessary for me to attend as well. I couldn't shake the feeling that this would be my last time I would see my beloved father.

I wanted to share my fears, but could not seem to get it out. Dad went into surgery with good spirits and we waited impatiently for it to end. The surgery went well, and the doctors informed us that the tumor would be sent for analysis and Dad would be taken to ICU. In fact, Dad was doing so well that Madonna and I had decided that we would return home the following day with some family who were coming to visit Dad in the hospital.

Even through all of this, my mind never wandered far from the pain I was feeling in my back. I remember praying that my back would hold up through the long drive from Rochester to Groton. The doctor called and updated us to Dad's status. He reported things were going well and they planned to give Dad some medications to relax so they could suction his lungs.

The doctors didn't know that Dad was allergic to Valium, and when the medication was injected, he had a bad reaction. He went wild, and the doctors were forced to restrain him in order to give him another shot of

Valium to further relax him, and unknowingly causing more issue with the allergy. All of this struggling caused a blood clot to form in his lung and eventually traveled to his heart causing a cardiac arrest, and Daddy died.

Dad's death was a shock to all of us. We were devastated, of course, and I was fully aware that my fear was confirmed. My brother, sisters and our families traveled back to our hometown to bury our beloved father and grandfather. It was a trying time for all of us, and through it all, my back continued to cause me much pain. And as it had always been, there was so much going on in our lives that I wasn't able to take the best care of me.

After the funeral, Mom called me daily crying. She was lonely and suffering severe grief. Even with all the family around, she felt empty without her husband. I felt so helpless and sad. I loved my dad more than words, and I wanted desperately to help my mom cope with her own grief. One day, when talking with her, I asked her to consider moving to Groton into an apartment. I explained that the kids and I would visit her as often as possible and keep her busy. She was ready for the change and agreed. Once again, this move was one that was setting me up for more and more support in my upcoming battle with cancer.

## PERPETUALLY ACHING BACK

The move from Watertown to Groton was one that had Mom torn. She wanted to move, but was hesitant to move away from the home that she and Dad had lived in together. She knew she would need to downsize and sell some of her things, but with some toil, she decided that the move was necessary and she needed to take the step.

Arranging the apartment in Groton took several months, and to make her move as easy as possible, Jim and I moved furniture, put away all items, and hung pictures on the walls. We even made her bed! All she needed to do was walk in! Within the first few weeks of living in Groton, she decided that she needed to visit her sister in Watertown. Again, trying to make things nice for her, I decided to paint her bedroom while she was gone.

It is strange what seemingly unimportant details a person remembers, but I remember that while painting Mom's bedroom a cancer insurance salesperson came to the door looking to sell insurance to me. I thought the pitch sounded pretty good and I called Jim to see what he thought. He decided that we couldn't afford anymore insurance at that time.

After Mom's move to Groton, I did everything I could think of to help her through her grief, but nothing seemed to work, and she truly mourned her husband until the day she died. I remember visiting her once very early in the morning. She was still sleeping when I came in, and when I came into her bedroom, she was clutching Dad's picture in her hand, holding it against her heart. I could still see her tears upon the glass that covered his face.

I realized then, that my focus on Mom's grief had truly kept me from working through my own grief for my dad. I knew that I needed to grieve for me. Grief is so difficult to talk about and not many really want to or know how to listen to another person's grief. Most of the time, we learn to grieve silently in our own way. For me, grieving meant remembering all the wonderful memories I had of my dad and my life with him.

Through tears, I remember Dad crying as the business he worked so hard to build, burnt to the ground. He had always been my hero, and I remember feeling that his tears somehow made him more human, and I loved him even more. Memories of Dad and the importance he played in shaping my life brought buckets of tears, but helped me to work through my grief after losing him. Now, I cherish Dad's life more than when he lived! He helped me learn and understand the strength that comes with the love of family relationships.

Although my own unexplained back pain continued, life continually moves forward. After Dad died, I was offered a new job with the Groton Schools, as their cafeteria baker. Boy, was I excited. I had always loved baking, and the kids at school were so much fun. After starting my dream job at the school, I learned that one of the patrons of the Cozy Cafe, an establishment I had worked previously, was the superintendent at the school. I remembered him frequenting the cafe for coffee and a roll.

I continued to live in constant pain and tried with all that was in me to be strong, but felt the new job was made for me. The kids were active and full of energy and I thoroughly enjoyed spoiling them a little by letting them pick out the roll or cookie of their choice. I was also ecstatic because I worked where my kids attended school, which was another way for me to be involved and I had the same schedule they did. I tried to see the positive in the job because I truly did enjoy it, but physically, I was continuing to decline. I was easily upset, which was a coverup for the pain.

Having a strong work ethic was something that I was, and still am, proud to have. I felt that it was not only my duty to demonstrate this in my new position because it was right, but it was also important for me to set an example of this for my children. I wanted each of my children to grow up and recognize the importance of hard work. But it was so hard to model this. I was in extreme pain and so tired.

Each day after work I would visit Mom and lay on her couch. She would rub my perpetually aching back. The words of the doctor constantly echoed in my mind, "Maybe it's in your head." Part of me wished I could just get over it, as the doctor suggested, and another part of me kept wondering how the doctor knew what my upper back felt like if he had fixed my lower

back. I knew I wasn't imagining the symptoms. I experienced back pain for over a year when Jim finally told me to make an appointment.
I scheduled the appointment for August. Jim went with me and helped me to explain my symptoms to the doctor. I told him of the back pain and recurring constipation I had been experiencing. He suggested that there was a possibility that the constipation could be causing my back pain. He wrote me a prescription for a controlled drug to take for the pain and a stool softener. I remember feeling extremely frustrated and upset with the doctor. I had been embarrassed to talk about the constipation, and throughout the entire appointment, he didn't examine me at all. He didn't look at my back, run any tests, or come up with any sort of treatment plan past the stool softener and pain meds. I was so frustrated and angry! Jim didn't know what to say.

The pain pills made it easier to work, but I needed to take double the amount to get through work. The pain was definitely improved, but I never made it through the day without pain. I often remember being stopped in my tracks with a jolt of pain and profuse sweating. The ladies at work noticed and asked if I was ok. I always covered, but it was such a lie. I hurt all the time, and I was bewildered as to why none of the doctors would take me seriously.

I found myself often sneaking into the restroom to take more pills and wash my face in cold water to slow the sweating. I tried to convince myself that I was getting a cold or had some type of infection, because I couldn't think of another reason for sweating as badly as I did. At night, I remember putting large bath towels in my bed so I wouldn't ruin the mattress, and at its worst, I was changing both the towels and my nightgown 2-3 times a night.

## PAIN AND PILLS, PILLS AND PAIN

I made several return trips to the doctor and told him that the treatment wasn't working. The pain was worse than it had ever been, and the constipation issues continued to get worse and worse. I treated the constipation with stool softeners, laxatives and enemas with no relief. Without concern, the doctor suggested that the pain meds were causing constipation. I reminded him that the constipation had been an issue before I came to see him, not after. He didn't budge. To say that I was frustrated is a gross understatement of how I felt. I hurt everywhere, experienced horrific constipation, and I was begging for help, but no doctor I had seen would listen to me. Still, the title of "doctor" was intimidating.

Through tears, I explained to the doctor that I hadn't had a bowel movement in a week. Although he didn't take the time to figure out my overall problem, he did make a plan to help me deal with the constipation. Still, I wanted to grab that doctor, pull his ear close, and scream, "My back hurts, and I am so constipated I can taste it." But I didn't. Instead, I made the trip over to the emergency room for an enema.

I was so embarrassed! I can only imagine being the ER doctor or nurse, waiting for a heart attack or an accident victim, and then being faced with a constipated mother of three, looking for relief from an enema. They were kind. They cleaned me out, but it wasn't easy. The nurses were surprised that I could stand all the pressure from the constipation. The nurse relayed that I should have been deathly ill.

Although the initial enema provided some immediate relief, it was only temporary. I continued taking pain pills, but the pain only increased. My appetite remained good, but I could not have any type of regular bowel movement. Laxatives, suppositories and enemas were my only relief from the horrible constipation. I should have bought their stock that year. Yet another visit to the doctor gave me the same diagnosis, more pain pills, and a return trip to the ER for an enema. Again, the nurse was shocked that I could withstand the pain and pressure of the constipation.

Those days were filled with pain and pills and pills and pain. I found myself relying on the meds more and more frequently. I continued to work, but it was all I could do to get through the days. Once at home, I would lie on the couch and beg for back rubs. Absolutely nothing seemed to help.

## THE "SPECIALIST"

As the pain increased and the doctors continued to ignore my symptoms, I felt myself getting increasingly frustrated and cynical. Finally, I was scheduled to see a "specialist" in November. At the appointment, I didn't even take my coat off. The gray-haired wizard came in right as I entered and said, "I want you to eat cracked wheat, fresh fruit, bran cereal, and come back in one month." It was all I could do to contain myself.

This guy was quite a "specialist". He never even asked me when I had my last bowel movement, which had been twelve days earlier, for the record. He didn't look at my distended stomach. He made no effort in gaining my history or seeking out why I felt it necessary to see him. This genius didn't know anything about me, but diagnosed and treated me without my participation. And, he wanted to see me again in one month.

Although I was so upset, I was determined to try anything. I stopped at the grocery store as I left town and purchased the ingredients for his prescribed diet. For the next month, I ate nothing but cracked wheat, fresh fruit and bran. I don't know if it was my diet, my horrible backache, or the BM build up, but I was not fit to live with.

I tried to stay positive and thought at one time that I was making progress, and then it seemed to stop. The month of November seemed to drag on for more like three months instead of one. I ate so much bran that I wanted to literally vomit all the time. Even baking began to smell bad to me, and that was a first, as I loved the smell of fresh baked cookies and bread.

Well, at the end of the month, I was back to the sophisticate's office for my number two appointment. My rectum was so tight it was like a drum. I couldn't even use a suppository. I did manage an enema, but nothing happened. I began to wonder where all the waste went and why my stomach hasn't just blown up? I knew I had to make this doctor listen to me, and I was ready to stand in the door and make him listen. He was going to hear what I had to say.

I entered the doctor's office and prepared myself to explain. I told him as calmly as I could, and he just as calmly said, "Barb, I have checked your x-rays and the blockage you have simply does not warrant surgery—it isn't significant enough for surgery. What you need to do is relax. Take a newspaper into the bathroom, sit down and relax!"

He's probably lucky that I didn't jump out of my chair! It was all I could do to maintain my calm and again, explained to him that I do sit! I continued that I sat a really long time, and it just does not work.

Then I received the crowning blow! "You just need to be potty trained," he replied and walked out.

I was so distraught! I cried and leaned on Jim asking him what we should do now. I felt so abandoned by the doctors. No one listened to me. Jim didn't know what to say either, and as he always did, said that we will just find someone else.

I was so miserable and continued taking more laxatives and every once in a great while I would go—big time. I would feel better for a few days until I began bloating again. I was so frustrated and helpless.

## THE APPOINTMENT

I was so miserable, but kept taking more laxatives. The occasional BM made me wonder if I had something out of line in my back, possibly the blockage the barium enema had shown. I was grasping for any straws because I was desperate for relief. Mom and I talked often when I made my afternoon visit, and she thought that since I found relief in a back rub that perhaps something was off kilter. We joked about getting old and wouldn't that be nice if that was all it was.

Throughout this entire ordeal, I tried my best to focus. I focused on work and my children. I tried to remember to thank God for my blessings, because even in my most miserable state, I knew I was blessed. I had the best family one could ask for, a husband I was sure loved me, and that is all one needed. It did help me through the toughest times, but my physical condition didn't improve.

While at work one day, I visited with my coworkers about what my mom had suggested. One of the gals I worked with said she saw a certain chiropractor and liked him a lot. After visiting about my bowel issues with her, she felt he could help. I was willing to try anything, so I called for an appointment.

Surprisingly, I was impressed with the chiropractor—he really listened. He suggested we get some x-rays. He worked on my entire body and put everything back in line. I was scheduled to see him every two or three days for heat lamp and ultra sound treatments. The chiropractor had asked more questions than all the medical doctors put together.

He wanted to know how I was sleeping, what my disposition was like. Was I perspiring at night, and did I still have problems with constipation?

I was a bit shocked by the questions, and I was so excited to answer them.
I hadn't been sleeping well at night. In fact, I had to stand in a corner to sleep. I explained how I would push my dad's recliner over to catch me should I fall. Adding, that every time I would get home from his treatment, laid on the floor and begged someone to rub my back, and that my mother

rubbed my back following work every single day.
The chiropractor, being wise enough to know his area of expertise told me that he could do no more for me because he felt that I might have an infection. Although I was faced with yet another crossroads, I thought maybe that I would finally be heard. Someone agreed with me! I had wondered about that too and no one had listened to me. I hoped and prayed that someone would listen to him.

I was able to go straight from the chiropractor's office to an appointment with a doctor I like to refer to as Mr. Clean. Once again, I was left with no relief. Rather than listening to my symptoms and devising a treatment plan that would find answers, he prescribed a back brace. Like the others before him, he didn't even examine my back.

I was so angry! I could barely contain my rage when I spoke. “I don't need a back brace, I came here for your expertise! I am 33-years-old and enduring more back pain than anyone could ever imagine.”

It didn't help. I left without answers.

My back pain made it impossible for me to move on. My daily functioning suffered, and I was miserable. Another appointment was scheduled, and I came in with a plan. I told him that I needed an appointment at the University of Minnesota Hospital. He didn't agree, but obliged. My hope was that if I went to the University Hospital that the doctors there would be professionals and maybe smarter than the condescending doctors I had been seeing in Aberdeen.

In the 1980s, appointments couldn't be made with a quick computer check. They required phone calls and referral papers and the process was quite slow. He explained that he would have his receptionist make the appointment and would have the appointment date sent to my home address.

Before leaving, I asked for a supply of pain medication, and he started writing the prescription and asked, “How many?” And once again, the doctor chose not to listen. I knew what I needed and he prescribed me half, with no refill. I felt sicker. And desperate.

And scared.

And angry.

And hopeless.

Worry compounded my backache. I knew I would not have enough pain medication, and the doctor wouldn't allow more. I paid the doctor more than I made each month, and in return he got richer, and I was only getting sicker and sicker.

I left in despair and thought only of the promised appointment. That appointment was truly the carrot that kept me sane. When it finally arrived in the mail, I nervously opened the envelope and saw the appointment scheduled for June fourth.

I cried!

It was mid-April. They had to be kidding. There was NO WAY I would survive until June. Miserable didn't even describe my day-to-day existence. I took as many pain pills as I could get my hands on—at least two pills every hour. I started with a prescription of 100 pain pills and wasn't able to get through a day without taking a good portion of my prescription. Every day. I had enough pills to make it a week or two if I forced myself to ration the prescription and suffer horrible pain.

But I tried to endure. I can't remember how many times I woke Jim in the middle of the night and begged him to take me to the hospital.

I know he was frustrated too. He would sound grumpy and asked if I was sure this time.

At that point, I became extremely frightened. I think my fear was largely due to the treatment I had received from previous specialists. They wouldn't take me seriously anyway, would they? They would chastise and belittle me. I would be made to feel like an idiot. Then, I would convince myself that I was feeling better and tell Jim that I would wait. Then, I popped a couple more pain pills and went back to the corner to stand, and hopefully rest.

My mood was awful! I felt crabby all the time. I doubt that Jim or anyone else understood how badly I hurt. I continued to work, but that was it. I could barely do that. The doctor bills were becoming overwhelming, and we needed my paycheck.

I couldn't do any work at home. When I got home from work every afternoon, I would lie on the couch in misery. The pain continued to increase. I knew it wasn't in my head. I was slowly coming to the realization that something had to be done.

The pain at that time was overwhelming. There are truly no adjectives to describe the torture I felt physically. Emotionally, though, I was just wrecked. Thoughts were slow to form in my brain, but when I could think straight, I thought about the present, the future, the past. I was angry and scared and anxious all at once.

I have to work, but I can barely stand. We need my paycheck, but I can't do it. I need to take care of my kids, but I can't function.

What if the doctor finds nothing?

What if he finds something?

How will I survive?

How will my family survive?

And so I prayed. I'm not sure that I even knew what I was asking, but I knew I needed the help of the Almighty. Please God, help me. The prayer for help was repeated over and over.

## UNBEARABLE PAIN

It was almost May. The superintendent called me into his office. I was nervous and wondering what I may have done wrong. Sitting in his big fancy office, I could feel my hands sweat. He looked at me and said, "I would like to send you to baker's certification school this summer." I was so excited and flattered, he saw my hard work and passion I put into my job. He also increased my salary that day and oh, how I could use that increase in salary.

Although I was excited about the certification course and extremely flattered about the pay increase, I soon realized that not everyone I worked with shared my enthusiasm. The women I worked closely with and whom I had always gotten along well, were suddenly irritable and angry.

I knew that my supervisor must be aware of the special treatment I was paid by the superintendent. My supervisor informed me that it was time that I would fill the supply bins by myself. Until that day, it was our normal practice to help each other emptying the 50 pound bags of sugar and flour. After that meeting, she must have felt necessary for me to suffer a bit, and I was expected to do it myself. I didn't complain, but I knew that it would be awful.

I was barely sleeping, and when I did sleep, I was standing in the corner. I actually couldn't even remember the last time I had slept through the night. I knew it had to have been at least two months or longer. I was downing handfuls of pain pills every day, and my misery seemed to compound instead of lessen.

Lifting the fifty pound sacks of flour and sugar by myself was torture. By the time I finished, I was dripping with sweat and hurting even more. But I was too stubborn to ask for help. Filling the bins by myself made me physically ill. On more than one occasion, the chore made me vomit.

After I came home from work, I was left with hours of pain. I tried everything I could for even a little relief. I sat until it hurt too badly to sit . Then, I would lie on the couch until that too caused so much pain that I finally had to stand in the corner to sleep. I always set Dad's recliner in the corner to catch me. When I woke up, dripping with sweat, I changed my night clothes, took some pain pills, and prayed for a little more sleep. If that didn't work, and often it didn't, I would walk and cry and walk some more.

Now, when I think back, I wondered what was I thinking about. I talked about my pain, but never really did anything about it. No one knew how bad it really was.

I spent my afternoons, miserable and suffering, and Jim seemed only to grumble about my not having dinner ready on time after his long day of hard work. I know he was frustrated too, and that he had no idea of the immensity of my pain. But I felt like he was ignoring me and my pain.

I remember telling my mom not to feel sorry for me if I die because at least I wouldn't be in pain. She heard me, but didn't do anything about it. Maybe she felt that I was exaggerating my symptoms. I don't know.

It's more likely that she didn't know what to do to help me, but it felt like she wasn't listening either.

The final straw came on May 5, 1984. I'm not sure what it was that sent me over the edge, but that was the day. There was nothing significant about it. It was just another spring day on the farm. Jim had gone outside in the early morning to do his usual chores when I pulled on my jacket and headed for the milking parlor. By the time I trekked across the yard and made my way into the barn, tears were streaming down my face onto the jacket and down onto my tennis shoes. My face was blotchy red and flushed with pain.

Between sobs, I screamed over the compression of the machines. Jim heard me loud and clear. My desire to go to the hospital had never interfered with Jim's work. I had never gone into that milking parlor or interrupted his evening chores, so he knew I meant business.

Jim agreed and asked if I could wait until the chores were done. Milk cows don't wait for medical emergencies. I told him I could, but I knew the next couple hours would be miserable. To pass the time, I went over to the big house where Jim's parents lived.

Jim's dad took one look at me and just said, "You look awful Barb. Don't you come back home til those doctors do something to help you.." I knew he loved me as he said, "Barb, I'm old and lived my life. I wish I could take this pain from you." I was touched by his words, but I also knew this pain was mine, and I needed to do something about it. Now.

I left Jim's parents home and went back to my house to wait. I took a shower and packed a bag, trying to keep my mind off the pain. Nothing worked, but I had to do something to pass the time. A few months earlier, I had started making a macrame hanging table. In desperation, I fell to my knees and started working. Anything to keep me from thinking about the pain.

Thoughts raced through my mind and I kept saying to myself, "Keep the pattern. You can do this. Keep trying." I felt like Dad was sitting beside me saying, "Barb, finish what you start."

I think that moment, however bizarre, was God's way of helping me survive. I'm not sure how I could've endured those long hours before Jim would be ready to take me to the hospital. So I moved my hands and focused my mind and I waited.

When Jim finally got into the house, he probably thought that I was making up my symptoms, until he saw my face. My hands were moving, and I was crying and shaking. He knew I was doing my best to keep it together.

We called The Family Clinic and were instructed to go straight to the doctor's office so that I could be helped more quickly. Before we left that morning, I called my mom and I told her that I wouldn't be coming back until something was done. For the first time, I felt that to be true. I had never felt that desperate for relief from the pain.

When we walked into the doctor's office, the receptionist asked if we had an appointment. I am sure she thought I was a hysterical hypochondriac, but I was in pain from the top of my head to the tips of my toes. I looked at her and simply said, "You have to help me—I hurt so badly."

She again calmly said, "Just have a seat, and I will talk to the doctor."
I cried and blubbered, "Sit? I can't sit—I can't lay—I can't stand—I can't do anything. I don't even want to live. Please help me! Please, help me."

With that, she went in to talk with the doctor and quickly came back, held the door and asked me to follow her. A doctor I had never seen walked towards me, and I suddenly knew that this was who I needed to see. I didn't wait a second. I said, "Help me please." This was all I could get out between my sobs.

He had intended for me to wait a few minutes, but quickly followed me into the exam room. They took my blood pressure, which was over two-hundred and forty. I heard the doctor say, "Take her to the hospital now!" He would phone orders to the hospital.

A room was ready for me when we arrived, and they administered shots for pain before my clothes hit the chair. Within minutes, I experienced the first pain-free moment I could remember. Suddenly, I had no pain. I felt warm and comfortable and totally relaxed. I was exhausted and fell asleep almost immediately. I slept soundly for three straight hours.

When I woke up, I felt great and thought, I can go home now. I didn't even feel sick; however, that feeling was short lived. The angry pain came rushing back, and it wasn't gradual like one might think. It came back with such intense force I felt like it was the worst pain I had ever felt, and I knew pain.

The intensity of the pain sent me straight to the bathroom. I fell down onto my knees with dry heaves. I pleaded with the nurse for another shot or pills or anything to help me be rid of this awful pain.

The nurse tried to explain that the doctor said I could have the shot every four hours, and I couldn't get another for an hour. I had lived a lot of long painful hours, but nothing was worse than that hour before I could be relieved.

The shots for the pain were the ultimate relief. The nurse would administer a shot, and I would feel so good. During the hours of relief, I could all but convince myself that I could go home and live my life. And then hour number three came, and the sky fell again.

## CANCER DIAGNOSIS

I had been in the hospital only a short time that I realized two things. First, my pain and frustration were finally validated. Second, I was sick. I didn't know what was wrong with me, but the doctors and nurses were finally looking to determine the source of my agony. One can imagine that the validation was a bit of a redemption for me. No longer was I looked at as a hypochondriac. However, the fact that the doctors finally believed I was sick was also a scary position.

Jim and I both knew that I would be staying in the hospital until a diagnosis was made. During the first few days, life at the farm needed to continue as usual. Jim came and went so that the milking chores were done and our livelihood could survive. My mom and sister-in-law, Eileen, both visited during the first days of my hospitalization, so Jim felt that he was able to come and go as needed.

The doctors finally determined that the best plan of treatment was to do exploratory surgery. They were operating with the expectation that they would find kidney stones. I was beginning to learn that once in the hospital, nurses and doctors asked the most intrusive questions, all of which would be repeated again and again.

The surgery was performed and everything went as expected, but they didn't find any kidney stones. Following the surgery, I half expected the doctors to blame me for the lack of findings. The doctor reassured me that he would keep looking and told me to hang in there. I was very unused to doctors listening to me.

At the time, I don't remember being at all concerned that kidney stones were not the culprit of my pain, but I vividly remember a strong desire to sleep. It was heavenly to just sleep. Relief from the pain was something that I had longed for and was finally able to achieve, if even for short bursts of time.

Later, after I had rested, the doctor and charge nurse came back with serious faces and asked to speak with me. When they came in, I was chatting and laughing with family and friends, feeling wonderful, on the good end of the pain shot. The doctor asked everyone to leave and when I suggested that they stay, the doctor insisted that he and the nurse speak with me alone.

It was as if time stood still at that very moment. I had known for a long time that something was wrong. I knew my own body. I felt the horrendous pain. I had prayed daily for relief, for as far back as I could remember. But this moment was different from all of those from the past. It was this moment when I knew the answer was finally found, and it was bad. I was entering my own personal nightmare.

The doctor and nurse sat on each side of my bed, both holding my hand.

"You have cancer."

Dumbstruck. There is really no word that can describe that moment.

Cancer.

The hubbub that followed was a bit more blurry. There were words that stuck out. Critical. No time to waste. Very sick. Serious. No time to waste.

I couldn't cry. I couldn't move. I couldn't even blink my eyes. I just stared at the clock on the wall. I have no idea how long it took for their words to sink in or how long I sat there in my own sort of trance.

I remember them asking over and over whether I was alright. I didn't respond for a long time. Finally, a tear rolled down my cheek, followed by more tears, and I was able to say, "I want my husband now."

He just held me close and the dam broke. That hug from Jim was never needed as much as it was at that moment. I was thirty-four years old with my whole life ahead of me. I couldn't have cancer. I had been begging for a diagnosis, an answer, relief, but cancer was not what I was expecting.

Other people have cancer, not me.

And, although the awful diagnosis was one that was as devastating to Jim as it was to me, Jim was able to remain calm and collected. He assured me with his quiet confidence that cancer was something we could face and get through, together. I trusted him.

Jim and I embraced each other as if our lives depended on it. Our hearts ached together. I clung to my beloved husband and trusted in his words. When that moment was over, I knew it was time to move on and face the world of cancer.

Once we had gathered ourselves together, we went together to tell our loved ones the horrifying news. They had all suspected the worst, and they were correct. There were tears and hugs and more tears. All told me of their love for me and their promise for prayer. My best friend, Julie, held me tightly in a hug, shared her love for me, and promised to help me through my illness. I knew she would. That time is imprinted on my brain as the day I entered hell, but I also remember my family and their cloak of love.

After the initial shock, the doctor needed to inform us of the treatment plan. The following morning, we were to fly to the University Hospital in Minneapolis, Minnesota. Treatment would begin once I was settled into the facility. There was a whirlwind of treatment terms and details and traveling itineraries. All I wanted was my children.

My children. Once the news sunk into my brain and I began processing the future, I realized that my children would be without me during the treatment. They might be without me forever. As numb as I was, my motherly clock clicked panic hours and minutes. I tried to soak up my children's presence like a sponge. I could feel myself missing them before I'd even left. That night in the hospital was so hard. It hurt with a physical pain, one that cannot be described in words.

I remember coming out of my room, my children at my sides, and rounding the corner to see Jim, our stoic rock, crying and pounding the walls in frustration and anger. Until that evening, I know my children had never seen their father cry. That night, I was without the physical pain that had been so debilitating, but instead had a pain in my heart that no amounts of medication could fix.

I felt as if I had entered the twilight zone.

CANCER!

We made it through that night, and when we woke the next morning, we knew we would face the day. Although it was fleeting, I know there was a longing for strength and survival.

The doctor came in with more information and a speech that still rings in my ears today. He told me that I would meet nurses that I knew were angels and others that may have trained with the devil himself. He told me that I would meet doctors that needed to go back to school for basic Tender Loving Care 101 and others who would touch my heart and I would feel their hearts breaking when they aren't able to take away the pain.

And he was right.

The enormity of the journey I was about to embark upon was one that I recognized and difficult, but I know that I didn't really grasp the reality of it at that moment.

## Barb's Journey by Barbara Pray

### HOUSE UPON MY SHOULDERS

The diagnosis of cancer relieved the persistent pain that brought me coming back to the doctor, but it was replaced with an invisible house upon my shoulders. I felt burdened and scared.

I already knew several four letter words, many of which I could've shouted in a barrage of anger. But a new four letter word had replaced all the others, TIME.

Every question was answered with a "wait and see" or "time will tell".

I pondered how much time and how little time I may have.

I tried to cherish the time I had.

I felt hurried and halted all at once. I felt empty, yet burdened with an immense weight. My shoulders ached, not with the physical pain I had been wishing away for months, but with emotional anguish. I needed help, wanted help, but there were no answers for me yet. I was lying in wait. Damn, time.

Everyone came to see us off at the airport, even my son, Kelly, who was supposed to be in school. The big "C" had hit him hard too. He had been in class earlier in the day, but walked out so that he could see us off at the airport. I had always known Kelly to be a great kid, but that moment was the first of many that demonstrated what a great man he was becoming.

We boarded that little plane, eyes blurred with tears and hearts so very heavy with sadness. I felt no pain, and I remember wishing that they could just keep giving me shots so that I could go home and be with my kids and live my life as usual.

I wondered if I would ever see my home again.

Why was this MY fate? Why was I the unlucky recipient of cancer?

## Barb's Journey by Barbara Pray

After our little plane landed in Minneapolis, a cab drove us to University Avenue. into an alley. With trash and boxes and pieces of outdated, rusting equipment standing haphazardly about. I remember feeling like I was part of a poorly financed gangster movie. This couldn't be the place. Surely, this is not right. My mind raced with anxious, scared thoughts. Why is this place so trashy? Does this cabbie know what he's doing? Why do we need to enter this place through the alley? This door needs painting. It is so dirty. What will it be like inside?

I don't want to be here.

I even remember asking the cab driver to wait. I was certain that this wasn't the correct location and I didn't want to be left without a ride.

The driver wasn't a novice and simply told us to go through that door and turn the corner. Show the staff your papers and they will tell you what floor you are to go to.

We thanked him, and I secretly hoped that he was wrong. But I knew he wasn't.

That was the door. My door. We walked in and the heavy, dirty door closed tightly behind us. Had I just been sentenced to death?

Once inside the door, the whirlwind began again. The receptionist checked my papers and directed us to the third floor. When she asked us if we wanted to take the elevator or the steps, I remember wondering if that rickety thing would make it to the third floor.

This is not what a hospital should look like.

Where were the shining floors and antiseptic clean smell?

Where were the bright lights and cheery staff?

Surprisingly, that elevator did make it and when the doors opened, there sat a blonde-haired man with a pony tail longer than my girls'. * Remember,

it was 1984. What kind of guy wears a ponytail? Answer: A guy named Tony, who turned out to be really nice. He did what he could to help me adjust to life at the University Hospital. That night, he took my papers and called me by name. I didn't want him to know my name. I didn't want him to say my name or to know anything about me. When he called me to show me to my room, the tears streamed down my cheeks. As Tony showed me my room, I saw my name on the door.

I didn't want my name on the door.

I didn't want a room there.

I felt I had just been found guilty and given a prison sentence, but no one told me what I had done wrong.

Like the back alley and the entrance on the first floor, the halls of the third floor definitely did not fit the description of a hospital. The halls were lined with carts piled high with gowns, masks and foot coverings. Every door had a cart. The carts were a hodgepodge of supplies. My children kept their things neater than those carts were!

A nurse, my first cancer nurse, came and gave me a pair of pajamas. I looked at those ugly, scratchy hospital pajamas with disgust and denial. I told her that I didn't want to put them on. I didn't even want to be there! I remember pleading with both the nurse and Jim to just let me go home.

Of course, I couldn't go home.

A bit after the nurse left, she returned to tell me that I had a visitor—it was my big sister, Eunice, who lived in the Minneapolis area. It was a friendly face and exactly what I needed, a little piece of home, but it gave me a reason to cry again. Eunice was my eldest sister that I looked up to. Having her here during this difficult time in my life brought me so much comfort.

Being admitted into the hospital, you always have the never ending paperwork. Eunice stepped into to help answer the 101 questions.

Question 1: What type of entertainment do you like? I snorted, and with a giggle said, "sex." My sister having my same sense of humor, actually wrote it down.

The answer to that question proved to be an ice breaker for every doctor that read my chart. They would often chuckle with my silly answer and learn that I had a sense of humor. That was often the starting point that established the doctor/patient relationship.

I didn't want to be in that hospital, but had never been treated as nicely as I was by both doctors and nurses, and that was very new to me. The building was less than desirable, but the people were beautiful.

## WORST DAY OF MY LIFE

I know I never truly understood what it meant to be alone until I found myself sitting in the cancer wing of a hospital, three hundred miles from home. I was scared, and after everything the doctors told me, I knew I was critical.

I was amazed how ancient their equipment was, for being such a well-known hospital. I commented on how crappy the accommodations at this hospital was. The nurse, who was taking my vitals, said, "the hospital is willing to use old things so that as much money as possible could be used for research to help beautiful people like you."

Wow! At that moment, I realized that I would have no trouble putting up with the green walls and ugly multi-colored drapes. Even the brown scratched bed table looked better. The room was really quite large, and there was plenty of room for a cot for Jim that the nurse brought in without even having to be asked.

When the doctor arrived, I recall thinking that he seemed calm and nice. He reassured me and told me that I would be kept comfortable over the weekend, not much would be done until Monday. He did say, "make sure to let the nurses know if you if you feel any changes."

I continued to receive my pain shots throughout the weekend, but the pain was steadily increasing. They tried to keep me comfortable, but couldn't. I was miserable. I spent more time in the bathroom with dry heaves than I did in the bed. That weekend was one of the worst of my life. The shots didn't even touch the pain, and I remember wanting to die.

My dear friend from Minnesota, LaDonna, had come to the hospital to visit that weekend, but I didn't even notice at first. I was either crying, writhing in pain, or totally out of my head. All at once. Jim was beside himself and didn't know whether I should see her. She was one of my dearest friends, who came by Greyhound bus just to console me. In the end, I did see her, and I'm glad that I did. That meeting was hard on us both, and we cried together. She had now seen me at my worst! She said, " I wish I could help you.." I said, "I just want to die". She said, "You can't die!". She was, praying for me in my time of need. This was the worst pain I had ever experienced in my life.

As the evening drew nearer, I felt sicker and sicker. I had dry heaves for what seemed like hours; they just wouldn't stop. At some point during the evening, Jim had to help me to the bathroom because my legs no longer held me. I began losing feeling in my midsection. I couldn't feel myself urinate. I could hear it, but I couldn't feel a thing. The fear overcame me because I didn't understand what was happening.

The nurse called the doctor at four a.m., and when the intern arrived, she was mad! She could not believe we awakened her for something she thought was so minor. She growled as she said, "It's no wonder you can't feel your legs. You are taking so pain many meds. It's the medication that is causing this." And then she ranted about being awakened for that.

Again, I felt like I was back in the doctor's office being disrespected. I felt weak, and once again, I was intimidated by the intern doctor. I was in extreme pain, so sick, and my legs were numb. I was SCARED!

I did make it through that night, but it was one of the hardest I've ever had.

Early Sunday, a new doctor came in. He was so pleasant and calm. He really didn't look like a doctor with his round face and thinning hair. He looked more like a grandpa to me. He wore street clothes and looked like he was ready to play golf.

He asked me to stand to see how straight I stood. I told him I couldn't stand and that my legs had gone numb around three o'clock in the morning. I remember him asking me to repeat what I had said. He asked why I hadn't called someone to help. I assured him that I had and what the intern had said. I have no idea the outcome for that intern, but I know I never saw her again.

The doctor began his examination by sticking my numb legs with a pin. He asked me to tell him when I could feel a sharp or dull prick in my legs. I was guessing, and Jim said I answered wrong. When the doctor was pricking above my waist was when I could finally feel the prick. From that examination, he wrote the order to see a neurosurgeon. Within minutes, the doctor and two neurosurgeons came in. They were very young and looked so serious. What was a neurosurgeon? I wasn't even sure what their specialty was at that time. Again, they pricked and poked. I was tired of the pricking and poking; just please give me something for all this pain. By that time, I was in so much pain, I was begging to die. The pain was more intense than any I had felt, and they just kept saying that I couldn't have anything for pain until they knew what happening with me.

The neurosurgeons came to the decision that they had to call the department head. I don't know how long it was before the two young doctors came back and brought with them two more doctors. The head neurosurgeon and another big wheel took their turns sticking my numb leg. They checked and rechecked records from my local hospital.

They still couldn't determine a cause, so they ordered a myelogram. I didn't even know what a myelogram was, but I did know a neurosurgeon had come to a cancer ward to conference with an oncologist, and this was not normal. I was beyond scared, fear and pain overwhelming my every sense.

I plead with everyone who came into my room to help me with the pain. All I could do was cry and beg. Although I'm sure they wanted to take away the pain, they had to figure out what was happening in my body, the doctor's wouldn't give me pain medication until they determined the cause of the numbness.

The doctors finally took me down for the myelogram. To perform the test, I had to lie over a round object with my back in the air under a screen that looked like a TV. They explained that they were going to put a long needle into my spine and inject some dye. Their hope was that this test would show them what was causing the numbness in my legs. I didn't care what they did to me as long as they did it quickly. There are really no good adjectives to describe the horrific state I was in at that time.

The procedure started with the doctors attempting to insert the needle into my back. I didn't think that the pain could possibly get any worse, but it did and I screamed. They weren't able to get the needle inserted correctly, but they continued to try again and again. I screamed and screamed louder and louder, until they were finally able to get the needle inserted correctly. It took them over an hour to get the needle inserted, and by then I was soaked with sweat from the pain, but they were able to insert the dye to see what was causing the numbness in my legs.

The dye went in and stopped in the middle of my back telling the doctors that there was no spinal fluid getting to my legs. The cancer was so large, it had wrapped around my spinal column and stopped the spinal fluid from flowing to my lower extremities. The dye running through my spinal column gave them the information they needed from the test, however; the procedure created a burning sensation that was excruciating. I felt like I was being burned at the stake. I was screaming so loud Jim could hear my cries down the hall.

With every level of pain I experienced from the first back pain I'd had, I always felt they couldn't get worse. As I began my cancer-fighting mission, I realized that I was fully mistaken. During each phase of treatment, I experienced a new level of pain.

Jim later shared with me that these times of pain were as mentally painful for him as it was physically painful for me. He felt helpless and scared and alone. He wanted to come to me and force the doctors to stop, but knew that what they were doing was necessary. He said he prayed and rubbed his cross so hard that he nearly bent it in half.

Once the neurosurgeon discovered the lack of spinal fluid to my legs, he went to Jim and told him that they would be taking me to surgery immediately to hopefully remove some of the tumor to restore mobility, but he made it very clear the urgency of the dire situation.. He gave us five minutes to say goodbye while they prepared for surgery. We were both so scared. Saying goodbye was so hard. I was worried about the state of my legs, but all I can remember about that moment was the overwhelming pain. I prayed that the anesthesia would rid me of the pain, if only temporarily". Jim shot me a thumbs up before they took me away.

I was taken into the operating room, and heard orders shouted and could see people moving. I was crying and hurting and trying to keep up with what the doctors were saying, but everything happened at lightning speed. When they came at me with a scissors to cut the beautiful night gown my mom and sister-in-law had given me, I stopped them. The nurses must have felt that I had a right to one last request, and they sat me up, whipped off the nightgown, and just as quickly placed a catheter and turbaned my head in what seemed like seconds.

I remember trying to make small talk with the anesthesiologist about it being a bummer for him to work on Mother's Day and him assuring me that I needn't worry. The doctor tried to lessen my fears by joking with me about my surgical turban, he said "you have the best Mother's Day bonnet of all. The whole time I kept praying to be relieved from the pain, and I didn't care how that happened anymore.

# SURGERY

I was wheeled into surgery at 5:00 p.m. on Mother's Day, 1984. I left my three beautiful children in someone else's care. I prayed simultaneously to both live and die. I didn't want to die, but I didn't want to live like this either. I couldn't live in the state I was in for much longer.

When I awoke from surgery, I was full of questions.

What day is it? What time is it? Where am I? Where is Jim? How are the kids? When can I go home?

The nurse was so amazed that I was so alert. She said that I should be feeling groggy and tired and all drugged up after everything I had been through.

Then I asked what I had been through? The nurse left the ICU room door open a few inches. I could see into the waiting area. I saw Jim, my brother, John, and my sister-in-law Eileen and my mom waiting anxiously to see me. I waved at them with my "Barb's Smile" to let them know that I was okay.

After I had gone into surgery, Jim had called home and reported the emergency surgery. With that report, my family had come to be by my side. They were surprised that I wanted to see them. They had been told I would be allowed a one minute visit per hour, if I could tolerate it. I was delighted to see them and everyone was amazed at how well I was recovering.

I felt like a new person. No, I felt like the Barb I was before I hit the ice. How are the kids? Please don't close that door. I want to watch my family! I felt so rested and in my mind everything was back to normal. I was well now—the pain was gone. My prayers had been answered, and I could go home.

I talked fast, like a child anticipating Santa on Christmas Eve. I heard them say, "Barb, you were in surgery for hours." I never heard eight hours. That's okay, I was out now! When would they let me go home?"

At 5 am, a new face appeared. His voice was one I recognized, but I didn't know the face. He grabbed my feet and said, "Can you feel that, young lady?"

I told him I could. One might have thought I had just given the Gettysburg Address as far as the doctor was concerned. He expressed that I was very lucky and that he hadn't expected me to ever walk again. Vividly, I remember his eyes filled with tears and his lips quivering as he told me that the team of doctor's had removed enough tumors to fill his cupped hands five times. And he added that they only scraped twenty percent of my spine.

The immensity of what he said at that moment still sends a chill. Twenty percent! Twenty percent in eight hours! My whole world came crashing down around me. Although it was obviously miraculous that I felt sensation in my legs, I felt the weight from that invisible house upon my shoulders. The reality hit me. I cried! I felt like I had lost complete control. And boy was I angry! Why me? Why didn't those doctors listen to me before I got this sick? This just wasn't fair. I knew my fight was just beginning and it was going to be a very long journey. It took awhile, but eventually I was able to pull myself together. I knew I had to just put my feet down and meet this head on.

Jim and I talked together and came up with a plan. We decided that our children, Kelly, Paula and Michelle, would stay on the farm with Grandma and Grandpa Pray so that they could stay in school. My mom agreed to help with the kids. Jim's dad and brother would take care of the farm and chores, and Kelly would help them. This would allow Jim to stay with me for my treatment and to continue to be my rock.

Kelly did receive an allowance for his contribution to the farm chores. We didn't know it at the time, but Kelly had informed his younger sister's that they were not to ask us, their parents, for money. They were to come to him, as we didn't need to be burdened for money.

With the plans laid out, my family was taking Jim for a quick lunch before returning to their home. I asked Mom to remind the kids that I loved them and missed them After they left, I checked every crack in the ceiling. The cracks looked like the Grand Canyon through my tears. I was alone and started digesting what the neurosurgeon had said, "You are a lucky lady—I never thought you would walk again." Until very recently, I hadn't ever contemplated a life without the use of my legs.

"You have large B-cell tumors that are fast growing." I wasn't sure I remembered correctly, but I thought he said that the tumors doubled every day.

"Five handfuls of tumor was only 20 percent."

I couldn't even pronounce it, and I certainly couldn't spell it. Yet I had it. He said that the doctor's thought I had non-Hodgkin's Lymphoma cancer when I arrived, and that my cancer had spread to my stomach, liver, spine and bone marrow.

I didn't fully understand what the function of most of those organs were. I was so confused.

I lay there mulling over all the doctor had said, and then needing to use the bathroom. I rang for the nurse and waited for her to come in. Without thinking, I swung my feet over the edge of the bed, and she was going to help me.

I should have seen a big stop sign flashing RED. I should've heard the screams in my head yelling, "Don't put your feet down."

But, I didn't see or hear anything. Really, the nurse should have known the do's and don'ts better than me, but that didn't happen either.

My feet hit the floor, and the pain shot through me like Grant hitting Richmond. Both of my hips lit up like Roman candles. The explosion just kept coming and coming—the pain was horrendous. I couldn't get back into bed fast enough.

Jim had been gone for two hours with the family at lunch. His heart was troubled, but at least, he was comforted by the thought of me finally not being in pain. When he entered our room, he saw me writhing in pain. He talked of that moment and many others where he felt overwhelming guilt. The "if onlys" crept into his brain. If only I had listened to you sooner. If only I had been more persistent in finding a good doctor. If only I had stayed today instead of going to lunch. Would anything be different?

We learned quickly that "if only's" aren't helpful. There is nothing that could be done about the past, and we had too much to deal with in the present to continue looking backward.

That night after returning from dinner, Jim vowed he would never leave my side again. Jim never wanted to ask the "if only" questions again. I had occasionally pondered the question as to whether Jim truly loved me. I had always been pretty certain that the answer was yes, and I knew at that moment, without a doubt, that the answer was a resounding and loyal, YES!

## SHINGLES

Recovery from surgery was difficult. Pain meds were once again on the forefront of my days, and even with the constant injections, the pain was still very much present. Without the pain, I could see the positive. I could push forward and be ready to get through the tough times. With the pain, I struggled so very much. All I could think was, "Why, Lord, why?" Once again, I just wanted to die.

I begged Jim to hold me, touch me, please don't leave me! The pain was horrific! Jim would always answer in his strong, calm voice, "Barb, we can make it through this. Just hang in there."

His voice.

I loved to hear his voice.

It was Jim's voice and constant support that got me through those times. I needed him like I needed air. Or pain meds!

My hours were spent waiting for pain meds and praying that they would just take the pain away for a little while. The doctor told me that the shots wouldn't help with the pain as they had before. It had been a grave mistake to stand on my feet. I was so upset by the mistake, and I knew that I was not out of the woods concerning whether I would walk again.

My prayers to God were ones of begging. Please, couldn't someone tell me how long before I would be well? What could it hurt for me to be happy, even for a little while? God, please, I am only 33-years-old, and my children need me. Lord, please help me.

Time, for me, both stood still and moved at lightning speed. I knew that the lives of my children continued without me. I knew how much I needed and wanted to go to them. I prayed for fast relief and long periods without pain. Days seemed to stretch into months, but continued to pass. Being in a hospital is almost like a time warp.

One day, on top of everything else, I began to experience a rash around my waistline, and it itched like crazy. I thought they had just given me something that I was allergic to, but the doctor's diagnosed shingles, a virus that is very contagious. To most, healthy people, shingles is painful and contagious, but not life threatening. However, in a ward filled with immunosuppressed patients with cancer, a virus like shingles could be deadly.

For me, shingles meant that radiation therapy had to be put on hold, and that was not a good option. My legs had started to feel numb again, and we knew that the tumors in my body grew at warp speed. The doctors decided that I could not wait any longer for treatment. Radiation needed to begin immediately.

What to do—what to do—what to do? Nothing in a cancer diagnosis is easy, but this seemed to be yet another insurmountable obstacle to overcome. But, the doctor's at University Hospital faced difficult decisions every day, and they were ready for mine. They knew that the shingles diagnosis must now fit into treatment. The doctor's put together a regimen of experimental drugs to help combat the shingles virus.

One day, a doctor who specialized in the treatment of shingles along with a posse of interns came into my room. I thought nothing of his presence, as I saw countless doctors and nurses and interns parading through my room all the time. While in my room, he asked to see the shingles and I obliged.

After he left, the entire nursing staff came running in all excited. "Do you know who came into your room?" I didn't. Excitedly, one of them told me that he was world-renowned for his studies in infectious diseases. I knew they were really impressed, and I tried to share in their excitement, but he was just another doctor to me.

That same day the doctors decided that radiation treatment couldn't wait and special arrangements needed to be made for me to receive the treatment. I couldn't have radiation treatments during the day because of the greater risk to the other patients. Instead, I would receive my radiation treatments at 2:00 a.m. And due to the shingles virus, the radiation therapy room would need to be sanitized daily after the treatments. I worried about the poor cleaning person who would have to hose everything down in the middle of the night, all because of me. But, the sterilization of the room was a matter of life and death, so it would be done.

The evening of my first treatment arrived, and I had just fallen asleep when an orderly arrived. It was 1:30 a.m. and he was so bright and sunshiny! Even Jim woke up bright eyed and bushy tailed. I suspect that Jim was feeling excited to begin the treatment that could lead to my recovery.

They put me on the cart toward the treatment room, and the orderly gave me a compliment that I still treasure. For so long, I had been in pain and feeling less than myself, to say the least. Looking good was not hitting the top of my priority list on most days. But that evening as he pushed me into my first treatment, he told me that I had the prettiest complexion. He told me that I was "just beautiful!"

That comment was probably just what I needed to begin looking forward, toward hope.

## RADIATION

The first radiation treatment was a strange experience! The doctors marked my body with an indelible pen. The whole time they were drawing lines, they were telling me what was about to happen.

Radiation treatments would be Monday through Friday at 2:00 a.m. I would receive five days of treatments and get two days off until I had completed all necessary treatments.

During the treatments, you must remain absolutely still. The treatment lasted a total of three minutes. All the treatments would be to my spine.

I was told that my skin would look burnt in the areas where the treatments were given, and that I might be sick to my stomach after.

I thought I understood everything, but depended upon Jim to remember all of it. The whirlwind of preparation finally wrapped up and I was informed that they were ready to begin the treatment.

Wow! Fear. Anxiety. Worry. I was left all alone for the treatment! Three minutes seemed to last an eternity! I prayed to God. I think my prayer that first night consisted of a repeat of, "please help me."

They were right. The treatment didn't hurt, but I did feel sick. That treatment was a rather embarrassing memory. I was the only woman in a room full of good looking men, and I started bleeding from one end and vomiting from the other. It was so horrifying! No one even blinked an eye. I was assured that this type of thing happened all the time and cleanup began without fanfare.

But it didn't happen to me. I felt like dropping into a hole.

Quietly—and I have never been a quiet person, we made our way back to my room. The continued vomiting didn't make a quiet procession easier either. The orderly escorting us to and from did his best to make me feel better, telling me that the residents are probably just thankful that they

aren't in my shoes.
I experienced dry heaves all night! Poor Jim, had to listen to all that and hold the bucket too. Neither of us slept all night.

My whole family kept up with the different treatments that were happening during my stay. My sister, Madonna, called the morning after my first radiation treatment. Unfortunately, I was still dry heaving and couldn't talk, but she wouldn't be deterred. Jim held the telephone to my ear and she prayed with me. I couldn't talk. I couldn't even listen. I just heaved and heaved but that didn't stop Madonna! She helped the best way she knew how—by praying!

Madonna prayed, and my thoughts wandered. I thought about all the bike rides we had together, her pedaling and me riding. Then I remembered her complaining as kids that she couldn't sleep while listening to me breathe. The radiation treatments were far worse than being kept awake as a child by my noisy breathing, but she stayed with me, praying me through the roughest hours, day after day.

From the second treatment on, Jim was my orderly. He was also my taxi driver, telephone holder, bucket wielder, and my life.

After each treatment, I was sick to my stomach. Jim held my bucket and wondered why I couldn't get something to help with the sickness. The third treatment was no better, but there was a a new twist--my legs were getting worse, not better!

The doctor's collaborated and decided that I needed to be moved back into the cancer wing where I would receive chemotherapy as well as radiation treatments. The outcome would be that I would initially get even sicker. I really didn't know how that was possible, but I was beginning to believe that I would most certainly be proven wrong.

I was moved back to the same room I had been assigned when we first checked into the hospital. The same nice orderly who had complimented me on my first trek to radiation was my chauffeur. I thanked him again for the compliment. I just hated the word cancer, and didn't want to face my name on the door of the cancer wing, but there was no choice.

## DON'T GIVE UP!

Although my days on the cancer ward was a time I'd just as soon forget, when I was feeling like a person, I did try to take time to think about and appreciate all the good things the nurses and orderlies had done for us.

The cancer ward staff was great! God gave them gentle hands and voices like angels. They gave me the ability to reach deeper into myself and draw out strength and the desire to live. They joked with us and tried to break up the tedium of the long, grueling days. When Jim left to eat a meal, he would often bring back candy for the nurses. They would joke about how fat he was getting from the delicious hospital food.

One day, the nurse's wheeled in a small black and white television set, and a recliner. Those little amenities were so appreciated. We'd been away from home for nearly a month when they wheeled it all into my room on the cancer wing. For most of that time, I was consumed with pain and treatments and recovery. Jim, on the other hand, was isolated from everyone and solely focused on me. I can only imagine how difficult his time at the hospital was!

Our one window overlooked the college campus. When we were sitting and passing time, we would look out and see people moving about and living their lives. We would always notice the weather, and it was summer. I remember longing to go out into the the sunshine—the beautiful sunshine. I had forgotten weather even existed.

I daydreamed while watching the young students hustle from here to there. They were the young doctors and nurses of the future. Jim and I wondered if they were expected to take a class in comforting families being torn apart by illness. We would entitle it, "Putting Your Feet Down—101."

I wouldn't wish cancer on anyone, but within days, I was certain that the doctors and nurses knew their field. My days of feeling small in the face of professionals was over. I received help without even asking. Being on the cancer floor, we no longer had long trips to the treatment rooms, and we even had a television and a window to entertain ourselves. The third floor, better known as the isolation ward, was where I spent my time during treatment. Mine was the floor lined with carts, heaped with gowns and masks. Those on my floor were in a more fragile state and needed the extra precautions of isolation.

My best friend's mother, also fighting cancer—lung cancer, was in the same hospital, only she was on the first floor. Her room looked much more like a prison with bars on the windows. The crime rate was high in the section of town where the hospital was. I loved Audrey, my friend's mother, like my own. I'll never forget the day she came to ICU on my floor. As they brought her through the third floor hallways, she was hollering that she needed to see Barb. They allowed her to peek her head into my room and she said to me, "You take care of yourself. You take care of yourself! Love you." It wasn't long after that when Audrey passed away from her own cancer.

Throughout my time at University Hospital, I had heard so many different medical terms and treatment options. I was utterly overwhelmed! Medical information is difficult to learn when one is not sick, and I was attempting to learn through pain. I did the best I could, but as always, I relied on Jim to keep things straight for me.

The charge nurse pushed me to become my own advocate. She suggested that we read a book on non-Hodgkins Lymphoma, the type of cancer I was fighting. As we read the book, we were not shocked to find numerous symptoms that were missed or ignored by my local doctors. Although the book didn't teach us everything we needed to know, we finally felt as if we weren't fighting this battle blind.

That same nurse also suggested that we continue to read my chart so that I stayed current on the different treatments. She continually told me that it was my right to know and that I should be included in the process. Both of her suggestions were really helpful to me, and hers was one that made me feel important in this journey, something that I hadn't always felt.

Once I started feeling better, Jim and I played Yahtzee, Cribbage, Bingo—anything to pass the time. We both were so homesick! The days seem to drag on.......... We missed our children the most, but we missed even the mundane parts of life. I missed baking bread and my home on the farm. Jim missed milking the cows and even missed cleaning the barn.

I soon became a pro at making it through the treatments. Following a chemo treatment, I would be sick for 4-5 days. I remember thinking to myself that I could vomit at home!

Each time we passed the sign which said, Municipal Cancer, I would wish to pull that sign off of the wall and break it into a million pieces. I wanted to go home. But, each time I saw that sign, I also became angry. My anger turned into determination that I would go home. Cancer would NOT kill me. I wasn't ready to die.

During our many hours of time together, Jim and I had serious talks. We were young, but we both grew much older in those weeks. We talked about our hopes and dreams and our children. I told Jim that I had to know that he and the girls would get confirmed, and they must attend church. I wasn't ready to give up and die, but just in case, I had to know their souls were safe. He said he would.

Jim would get me to talk every day and make me think about something. He always kept me positive and happy—future thoughts. During that time, we each became very aware of our marriage vows. The day we were married, we spoke the words, "in sickness and in health, til death do us part". The day we were married, I'm sure we spoke those words in confidence, but I doubt that the young Jim and Barb could've believed the test that those vows would take. Thankfully, we passed that test.

Neither of us was ready for death to tear us apart, and neither one said a thing about that. Jim never allowed me to think about death. Positivity was our focus and our stronghold. Jim's mantra during that time was always, "don't give up." He prayed his mantra and rubbed that prayer cross. I know God heard him.

## WILL I LOSE MY HAIR?

Chemotherapy treatments were harsh. The medications made me vomit for days, and just when I was beginning to feel better, I would receive a new batch of the medications. It was bad enough having to be sick, but I didn't even want to consider being sick and bald.

I was told that I would lose my hair once I began chemotherapy treatments. There was no way to avoid that, but in my own mind, I had convinced myself that I would be a rarity and keep my hair. I went down to the scarf and wig room—just to look and to appease those around me. The wigs all looked like something one would wear at Halloween. I did pick out a couple scarves—not that I would need them.

Even then, I knew that my belief that I would not lose my hair was a bit skewed, and that I probably should have just taken them at their word, but I remained in denial. I had no intention of losing my hair, just one more piece of me. I didn't want to let go.

Throughout my stay, Jim had always been my main nurse. When I didn't know what to do or how to handle something new, he would call for help. It seemed to work for the nurses and for us. One morning, Jim helped me to the bathroom so that I could clean up. That morning, I didn't want to brush my hair. I was afraid of losing it. I always had thick, pretty hair, and I knew it would soon be gone.

I grabbed hold of the side my head and my hair just fell into my hands. I hadn't lost just a couple of hairs, I lost half my head of hair. I cried and cried as I pulled the rest of my hair out. Then, I stood and looked into the mirror at baldness. And I cried some more. I couldn't even look at myself in the mirror. How would I ever be able to go home to my children looking like this?

Jim must have realized what happened, but he wasn't about to force me into coming out. He knew me well enough to know that I would come out when I felt my feet firmly planted on the floor and I was ready to face the next hurdle. It took awhile, but I eventually requested Jim to get me one of my scarves. He handed the scarf to me through the crack I made in the bathroom door. I didn't want him or anyone to see my bald head. Jim never said a word about my hair. He knew how difficult this step was for me.

Once starting chemotherapy, my appetite was bad. I loved to eat, and wondered if there would be anything that I could even stomach. As it turned out, breakfast was the one and only meal I could even stand to smell, let alone eat. Of all things, oatmeal and cream of wheat were all that I could choke down, but I had to force myself to eat because I just wasn't hungry. The smells from the trays of food being delivered was too much for me. I would have Jim close the door to my room to so I couldn't smell the offensive odor of cooked food. Even then, I often was forced to grab my bucket and vomit.

The doctors and Jim pleaded with me to eat. They offered me whatever I wanted. One day, I thought a BLT sounded good. After just a few bites, I had to reach for the bucket. On other occasions when I thought of something that sounded good, I would start to eat and fall into a deep sleep before I swallowed the first bite.

Food! I loved to eat! What was happening to me? I knew I had to eat to keep my strength up, but I just couldn't! Instead of thinking about food and the smell of food, Jim and I would look out our window and try to enjoy every sunset and sunrise—to me it meant the passing of time. We would check the weather report, even though neither of us felt the presence of wind blowing upon our faces or the warm sprinkle of a summer rain shower.

We anticipated Sundays like spoiled kids. Remember, 1984 was in an era before cell phones and constant communications. For us, Sunday was the day we set aside to call home. We would call and try to sound upbeat. We treasured our talks with them, listening to their lives go on without us. After our conversations ended, we cried like babies. They were never to know how we suffered. We wanted them to know that we were fine, but we missed them terribly.

On one particular Sunday, seven weeks after I'd checked into the hospital, I was able to tell my children that if my white blood cell count was up, we would be coming home after the next chemotherapy treatment. I was so excited! On June 21st, we were discharged to go home. I had dreamed of this day for weeks, and at many points during my treatments, I didn't think this day would ever arrive. I would get to go home and be with my children. God did hear my prayers!

The seven weeks in the hospital were the hardest of my life. I remember how much pain I had when I came into the hospital and how much more I had suffered during the treatments. But I survived it all.

I knew that leaving the hospital that day did not mean that I was cured. I knew my battle was far from over, but I was ready to take the gift. I got to go home. I would see my beloved children. I was never so happy as I was at that moment.

I do know that God was with me every step of my journey. Not only had I survived the grueling seven weeks of treatment, but I was going home, without a wheelchair. I would be walking out with the legs that just a few short weeks prior weren't strong enough to hold me. The doctors told me that I was one lucky lady, I don't think that luck had anything to do with it. God walked me into the UM Hospital just in time to save my life and legs and God walked me out.

That week of waiting, knowing that our exit was close, seemed to stop time in its tracks. Our mail became more important than ever. We read and re-read every card, every verse that had been written. We talked fondly of our friends and acquaintances as we read the cards that were sent. Every day was marked the days off on the calendar, one half day at a time. Every mark put us a little closer to check out time.

At home, the girls cleaned the house, and my mom cleaned the carpets. The kids hung welcome home banners for our arrival. I know that they were more than ready for their mom and dad to come home. They were hoping, as were we, that everything would go back to normal.

Before leaving for home, Jim had to retrieve our car from the patient parking lot. Until leaving was a reality, we hadn't thought of our car. We counted our money, just $60 between us. The parking lot charged $5 per day, and we had been parked there for 56 days. Our total bill would be $280, an amount we just didn't have.

Although he wasn't hopeful in retrieving our car from the lot, Jim went anyway, hoping for a miracle. He drove the car to the window and the attendant charged him five dollars. Jim was dumbfounded, but ever so thankful. Five dollars! We were both certain that God, in all his mercy, had been there for us once again.

When check out time finally came, Dr. Jim, as he was fondly known, was given detailed instructions for my medication regimen. He was prepared to administer pills. Some were every four hours and some were twice daily. By the time we left, the medication regimen was a piece of cake for Dr. Jim. He'd seen almost everything!

Much as we both disliked that prison and all it stood for, we cried tears of thanks and love for the people as we hugged and said our goodbyes. The people who worked inside the drab and ineptly furnished building were my saviors. Without them, I wouldn't be going home.

I was discharged until the next chemotherapy treatment, a week and a half after my release. It was imperative that I not miss that treatment or any others for that matter. We knew our orders and were ready for home.

With bucket in hand, Jim helped my weak body out the door. We both felt like freed prisoners! The sunshine felt so good on our faces—it was so warm, and the wind was so refreshing.

I couldn't explain it, but I wanted us to drive out of our way to see my sister, Eunice. They lived in Minneapolis and I needed to thank her for her hours of prayer. During our quick visit with Eunice, the first four hour medication was due to be given. As Jim drew the first shot, a case of nerves set in and he dropped the bottle. We managed to save most of it, but there wouldn't be enough to get us through until our return trip. He gave me the shot and called the University Hospital to explain. They called the prescription into Sioux Falls, and a man would personally drive the medication to us.

The trip home took six hours, and it was difficult. Jim drove and I lay on the back seat like a. well loved rag doll. I was crying with both excitement and fear. I was fearful how different I was physically and emotionally from when I left 8 weeks before.

During my hospitalization, I lost thirty-five pounds, but my face was puffy from all the medication. I struggled to think clearly, and I didn't want anyone to think I was " drugged up", but in all reality, I was. Just before turning onto our gravel road, Jim stopped and told me to pull myself together. He said," We needed to stay strong for the kids". I quickly dried my eyes and did my farmer best to blow my nose before we started on the last road to home.

My children were waiting eagerly for the first sign of dust on our country road. When we drove onto our farmstead, all three were jumping and waving as only kids can do. It seemed to me that they had grown six inches or more in just 2 months!

They were excited for me to come into the house and see how they had taken care of everything. The house was spotless and the mirrors were shined and the laundry washed, dried and put away. I saw the welcome home banner, and I was so very proud of them. Then, I saw the truth through their eyes. We were their parents, and they loved us! It didn't matter to them that I wore a scarf on my head and had a puffy face. I was their mom, and I was home. I was weak, but they could help me—just be their mom.

I will treasure that first night's homecoming more than any other. Being home again felt awesome....... From that day, 2 months prior, when Jim first drove me to the Aberdeen hospital that started this journey, I wasn't sure that I would ever see the most beautiful place on this earth, my home, filled with my family. But I made it back to the people I loved so dearly, and that is the greatest gift.

As we got settled into our life at home, our family and friends were so good to us. People brought us bags of groceries and stopped for visits. My best friend from high school Julie bought me a really nice wig. Weak as an old dishrag, I took that wig into the bathroom, pulled off my scarf and looked into the mirror. I placed the wig on my bald head and I saw myself as a person again, and I liked it! That wig made me almost feel like myself again.

I just couldn't get enough of my children. I wanted so much to be the mom, the Barb, that I had been before cancer had taken over my life. With my new wig and makeup and my flash of the Barb smile, I could fool everyone—even my mom, at least for awhile. I was super sensitive about everything, and I wanted to be alone with my family.

Each morning, Jim carefully placed thirty-two pills onto the counter. I needed to take some every eight hours, some every six hours, and others every four hours. Jim set alarms for each set of pills and when the alarm rang, I took the meds.

When we were home, Jim worked hard on the farm to make up for lost time of being away.. He wanted to do what he could to repay his brother for the work he'd done to keep the farm running during our absence. He knew he had future debt to pay as well, knowing we would be gone more than a week of each month with my continued treatments. He worked endlessly between the farm, caring for me and finding his time to spend with his kids.

## BILL COLLECTORS

Once we returned home, the hospital wasted no time in sending bills. Several even beat us home. Everything had been sent to the farm, and the kids dutifully put them in a neat pile on my desk. I dreaded opening those bills. I knew we had little money to give them.

Our deductible had been met before I ever entered the University Hospital with cancer. The insurance covered eighty percent of the bills, which left twenty percent for us to pay. Most of the pile on my desk were bills from the area hospital, and we had already passed the sixty day 'grace' period, as if that mattered.

The total monthly income at that time was approximately eight hundred dollars a month, depending upon the highs or lows of the milk production. Without my paycheck, our income was even more meager than it had been previously. It seemed impossible to comprehend how we would pay all the medical bills, and that didn't include our cost for medications, which totaled more than our monthly take home.

I knew I had to open them and find out the damage. I opened the bills one at a time. One bill and I nearly passed out. That one alone was fifty thousand dollars! The bill collectors began calling before I could muster the strength to open the rest of the envelopes. Friends would often call to wish me well, and bill collectors called for their payments. In the age before caller ID, answering the phone was kind of like playing a game of Russian roulette. If I were lucky, a friend would be on the line, if I were unlucky, a bill collector looking for something I couldn't provide.

We didn't have any money, and it didn't matter how much we tried, we would never be able to give the bill collectors their fee. When I answered the ring and a bill collector was on the line, the best I could do was promise that we would pay, eventually. They would get nasty with me, pushing and pushing for payment. I always wanted to respond in kind, "like I chose to have cancer."

I was very sensitive, between my weakness, fighting cancer, worrying about money, and trying to stay strong; any little thing would throw me over the edge. My mother and some of my friends came to visit and help out. I was wearing a scarf, and as my mom passed behind me, she accidentally pulled the scarf off my head. I blew up! She didn't understand why that upset me so badly and tried to make light of it. She said something about seeing my bald head as a baby and it wasn't a big deal then either. To her, it wasn't a big deal. To me, it was. I didn't want anyone to see me with a bald head.

During my time at home, I spent most of my hours in an easy chair or on the couch with the girls getting instructions as needed. Michelle was my eleven-year-old chef, and she eventually learned to be a really good cook. I always worried that she might get burned carrying liquids, but she never did.

Paula was twelve, and she cleaned our home. We spoke often about when they were younger and complained about getting up on Saturday mornings to do housework. Then, when I was unable to contribute, I was glad that I had taken the time to teach them—they became excellent helpers for me. Thank you, girls!

## TWENTY-FIVE POUND PIGLET

The support we received from our friends and family was overwhelming. We were so very humbled and thankful for all of the love we received. One of the local farmers built a new machine shop and was planning a barn dance in the new building before moving the machinery into it. He called and asked if we would allow him to raffle a piglet to help us with our travel expenses. Of course, we agreed.

As I readied myself for the the barn dance, I did my best to put on my "Barb" smile. I repeated Jim's stern and serious words in my head throughout the entire event. "Barb, you can do this—be strong."

Later, I looked at the little piglet that was to be raffled off for us, and I thought, "Pig, you weigh all of twenty-five pounds, and you have more strength than I have." I was thankful for that pig! The money provided for us by that little piglet gave us a working fund for our trips back and forth to the hospital. I don't know what happened to the piglet, but I do know that little pig did a very good thing for us. We were introduced to the reality of good friends and generous hearts.

That night I made a short thank you speech to the friends and family who were there supporting me. I remember my resounding message. "I am going to make it. Thank you for your love and support." And I knew that I would. My feet would hit the floor and I would find my strength to endure.

Following the barn dance, we received $1500 to assist in our travel expenses to and from the University Hospital. And that money was given to us just in time for our first trip back. During our time home, we mastered the dispensation of all thirty-two pills. Twelve pills every four hours, the pain pills, the pee pills and whatever else was in my weekly pill list, all of which cost more than our monthly income.

We avoided talking about what lay ahead. I worried about that first trip back, but I didn't want to talk about it. I was so scared, but I couldn't let the kids know how fearful I really was. I didn't want them to be afraid for me or think that I would not be coming back home. I often wonder if maybe I should have been more open about everything that was happening to me, but with Jim and I gone so much, I just felt this terrible illness might be too much for them to handle.

When it came time to leave, we put our suitcases into the car. My stomach muscles were tight, my head ached, but I could not shed a tear. I forced myself not to cry. No tears! I held firmly to that thought while Jim drove out of the driveway. I lay on the back seat smiling and waving and blowing kisses while tears were welling up in my eyes and I bit the inside of my lip to keep from crying.

Once the dust of the road swirled behind the car, we no longer could see each other, and I couldn't hold back the tears. Reality—we both knew what lay ahead. Jim just let me blubber away; he wanted to cry too, but knew one of us had to be strong.

The weather was nice, and the trip to Minneapolis, under any other situation, would have been a ball. The trip into Minneapolis was somber. As we made the last big curve into the city, and my tears started again. I didn't want to be there! I didn't want to have cancer!

The anger surged as we drove into the city for my chemo treatment. I remember thinking bitterly that I hoped the doctors that didn't listen to me were able to live with themselves. I wondered if they realized what great pain and hardship they had caused me. Not to mention the amount of money it was taking to treat the illness they had said was in my head.

I wanted to go home and be with my kids, not to be driving into the gangster-like alley to take another treatment that would make me deathly ill.

As always, Jim was calming when I needed him to be. He just repeated to me that we would be home in a couple of days. The kids would be waiting for me.

The nurses were expecting us and had prepared the room with the television and Jim's bed. In return, Jim brought a big supply of candy Dots to share with the nurses.

The chemotherapy treatments were long and hard, but I praised God when my white count stayed within the normal range. That normal test meant that I would go home again! We felt like that little piglet had kissed us as we checked out that time. The neighbor's benefit money made this trip worry free, and that was the only worry free thing in our lives at the moment. We were thankful for the small things.

The drive home was exciting! Jim drove and I vomited. I am certain that Jim enjoyed every mile. I couldn't wait to see my kids.. I knew it had been only a few days, but I loved and missed them so much. It was always in the back of my mind that I might not have enough time with them. I might not see them again.

The treatments continued to make me sicker than previous ones, and I didn't think that was possible. Regardless, we did manage to keep how very sick I was from the children.

When we were home, Jim put out piles of pills and set the timers for each dosage before leaving to milk. Jim was so busy wearing the hats of both Farmer Jim and Doctor Jim. When we were away, Jim's brother took care of the farm chores. Upon our return, he took time off until we needed to leave again. Jim worked so hard!

It wasn't anyone's fault, but often friends and acquaintances would speak of the chemotherapy trips as if they were a mid-month mini-vacation. I would have traded places with any one of those silly people in a heartbeat. Cancer treatments were the furthest thing from vacation I had ever experienced.

I realize that none of these frivolous comments were meant to be offensive, but I was offended, none the less. I would never have wished my illness on anyone, but I would have enjoyed some time off with our kids. But fun times were never discussed. Our lives revolved around cancer during our treatment "vacations" and the farm when we were home.

## CHEMOTHERAPY TRIP

Our week and a half at home seemed to be but a blip of time while our chemotherapy trips seemed to drag on forever. It often seemed that before we even unpacked our suitcases that it was time for the next treatment. I felt I was getting stronger and I was hopeful for a complete recovery; however, the chemotherapy treatments seemed to just go on and on......

A friend called me and asked if I would be offended if they had a benefit for me. I reminded her that the neighbors had already had one but, gave the ok for yet another outpouring of support.

When we returned home, we learned that the City of Groton would have a street dance and auction off items that they had gathered from businesses. The event was to be held on my birthday. I was overwhelmed by the communities support.

Someone paid one hundred dollars for a twenty-five foot extension cord that he didn't even need. My brother purchased a pendant necklace for sixty five dollars, and then, he gave it to me. The emotions and love that I felt that evening were so welcomed. It was a wonderful night, and I saw friends that I hadn't seen for months. It was difficult for me to accept that they were there for me, but they all were.

By ten o'clock, I was exhausted, but I needed to thank them. Jim helped my limp body to the microphone and I flashed "Barb's" best smile. I told them that they had given me my biggest and best birthday party I'd ever had! I thanked them for coming to my thirty-fifth, and added, "Lordy, Lordy, I'll see forty." It was my battle cry for the evening! They all laughed, and I was certain that the noise could be heard for miles. I left that evening more tired than I had ever been and full of excitement from the night's activities.

That evening gave me an infusion of determination like I had never had before. I thought about all that happened at the dance and auction. People I barely knew expressed admiration for my faith and perseverance. I felt humbled and blessed to have so many wonderful friends. Grown men cried as they shook my hand expressing their wishes that I would be healed. All repeated the message that I should continue to fight.

As I pictured in my mind's eye, our friends walking door to door asking businesses for items to auction off for my benefit; my heart felt warmed and I was encouraged. My friends that came to the benefit will never understand what strength and courage they gave to me that night. I knew that I had to be strong and get well—I didn't want to let them down!

Once home for the evening, I was exhausted but excited from all of the activities of the evening, so much that I couldn't sleep. I remember walking through the farm and sitting in my dad's swing. During difficult times, I had often spent time contemplating life and praying. There truly is nothing more tranquil than the stillness of the country and a familiar place to help a person find her center.

As I sat on the swing that night, the night so still I could hear my own heartbeat. I remember praying, "Who am I, God, that you are mindful of me?" The answer was the night breeze as it caressed my tear-stained face. That small sign was my assurance of recovery.

I thought about that evening and was shocked by the number of people who shared that they were praying for me. I had heard stories about how my disease had affected my siblings, my mother. I knew my family was concerned for me, but I didn't realize until that evening how great that concern was.

I made my way back into the house in the moonlight; alone and weary from the busy day. I was mentally drained from living and reliving not only this day, but parts of my childhood, too. It was hard to put into words, but I had a comfortable peace that I knew only God could provide.

## CHEMOTHERAPY AT HOMETOWN

Chemotherapy treatments were going well, and the doctors in Minneapolis arranged for me to have the next chemotherapy treatment in my hometown medical facility. I was pretty excited to skip the long drive to the cities. I was much stronger emotionally than ever before. My family doctor, that diagnosed my cancer, stopped by before the treatment and told me how proud that he was of me and to tell me that he had visited with the other doctors that had treated me (poorly), and had let them know without hesitation how they blew it with your diagnosis and I had suffered because of them. It was a small consolation prize, but it was appreciated.

Jim took me to the room the hospital designated as my chemotherapy room and we immediately realized that they did not know how to give me this type of treatment. Jim had to show them what to do. Looking back, we should probably have stopped the procedure immediately, but we didn't.

The nurse proceeded to put the IV into my arm, and it felt okay, but the needle had completely missed the vein. I had finished the treatment and was on my way home before anything became evident. The five harsh, chemo drugs were being pushed into my arm, not my bloodstream. My entire left arm had begun to swell and was turning purple. I didn't realize at the time how significant the messed up treatment would be!

After the chemotherapy incident, the kids and I were traveling to see our Minnesota friends We started our trip with an evening meal with our friends. We rejoiced, thanked God, laughed and cried. We compared our children's growth and ate a really delicious meal. Seeing all of them was great, but never once did I mention that my arm was hot, painful and very uncomfortable.

My sister, Madonna, invited my family to attend a ministry camp at Strawberry Lake. They thought it would be good for me to relax and just hear God's Word for a few days. She assured me that we would like the cabin on the lake and that it was a beautiful place, and she was right!

Madonna and I really enjoyed sitting by the water, listening to the sermons.

I thoroughly enjoyed being with healthy people. One of the ladies at the camp gave me a Bible verse Mark V:36, "Be not afraid, only believe." I kept that verse as my own, and I return to it whenever I need to remember.

Once everyone had gone to bed, I called Jim and told him about my arm. He felt it necessary to call and confer with the doctor's at the University Hospital, and he was right. The following morning, Jim came early to get us so that I could go to Minneapolis for another treatment.

The cancer doctor took one look at my my arm and had a fit. My left arm had been burnt by the incorrect IV placement, and would never accept an IV again. He would not send me back to the local hospital again, and I didn't argue.

The trips to Minneapolis were becoming more and more difficult, not just because of the time away from the family, but because of the increasing number of bills. We had so many bills that we simply could no longer talk about them. I looked at the mail, but we did not have a dime to pay any of the bills.

I felt responsible for everything, but helpless at the same time. The telephone calls from bill collectors came frequently and the collectors were beyond rude. Each bill collector thought theirs was most important, even more important than feeding and clothing our children.

We scrimped enough money to put gas in the car for our trips. The tires were bald, but we couldn't afford new ones. We tried to pack lunches to go when we made the trip to Minneapolis, but they were always cold and tasteless. On the return trips, we simply would not eat.

One of the hungry trips home, we rounded a bend in a small Minnesota town where the highway cuts right through the residential area. On the corner was a large beautiful home, and we saw people running and laughing. A picnic table, laden with food, stood in plain sight.

## BLACK ICE ACCIDENT

Those months of treatment left both Jim and I feeling helpless. We never discussed money because we had none. We tried to avoid any topics we could do nothing about. We both felt out-of-control about almost everything.

We knew the kids needed us, but their needs could no longer come first. Jim needed to work the farm, but that was not the priority. What came first were the trips to Minneapolis and cancer.

It didn't matter what type of weather was forecast, we needed to leave when it was time for my chemotherapy treatment. We drove through thunderstorms, lightning and hail—this probably wasn't the smartest, but we had to go--I could not miss a treatment.

We were trying to teach our children to think and reason through things, but the whole time Jim and I were doing things that completely contradicted what we were saying. And I just knew that I was to blame for all of this!

I would get down on myself because I wasn't able to work and help to pay all of these bills. Work, I couldn't even take care of myself.

The summer trips for treatment continued to sneak up on us and turned to fall. Each time, we repeated the process like pros. Drink the nasty peach chalk drink before the CAT scan, get the scan, have the treatments, barf a lot, and head for home..

In October, winter hit weeks early, not typical for South Dakotans or Minnesotans. Trees were laden with horrible frost and ice. We drove on treacherous black ice for miles. Headlights coming towards our car would blink at us because of the glare of the ice. We dared not go faster than 35 or 40 miles per hour. I remember Jim saying that he didn't think the people in the other car knew they were driving on ice. It was then that we saw taillights become a brake light. Their car lunged across the highway hitting an oncoming car head on. They hit so hard that we could actually see them bounce off each other backward, and then, both sat on the highway still. Windshields were broken, doors torn off, engines pushed into the front seats and bumpers lying on the highway. Their were bodies slumped over the steering wheels. We passed them by several hundred feet before we got stopped, and knew what a miracle it was that we hadn't hit anything on our passage through.

When Jim got back to them, others were stopping to help. The sight was troubling, but we knew that we had been given special guidance through the debris on our bald tires. We prayed for those involved in the accident, we never did find out their fate, and we thanked God for sparing us.

## SHADOW IN MY STOMACH

Jim and I often did silly things to pass the time during the long trips to the hospital. We always looked for the wooden fence. It was a spot of fencing that had been under construction for several months. It was the kind of fence that was eight feet high and built a section at a time, except for one section, the section we looked for during every trip. We finally came to the conclusion that the owner had run out of money and was buying the remainder of the fence, one board at a time. It became our habit to check the fence every time we drove by.

Whatever joyful moments we had driving to Minneapolis, the mood quickly changed as we made the curve into Minneapolis. Reality set in and the weight of the invisible house once again lay upon my shoulders. Then, that awful door was before us and once again, I would have to enter and use that ugly elevator and go back into the world of isolation.

The world of cancer and its victims always caught in my breath and heart as I looked into eyes of sadness. I watched the weak shuffle and ache with pain as they moved. There were wheelchairs and gurneys piled high with gowns and face masks. I didn't want to be here, I was certain that I didn't want to live here, but I knew without a doubt that I wanted to live.

I had been coming so long that I began to recognize people by their first names. I would see the scarves covering heads in place of lost hair. I would see friends who had been through difficult treatments and thank God that he or she had lived another 10 days. I no longer thought about time in years, months or even weeks, my thoughts were for the moment. I wasn't always certain that I could even count on having today, so how I spent my time began to really matter to me.

That year, we celebrated the start of school with a trip to Crazy Days. We couldn't afford much, but the time with the kids was great fun. As much as I could, I tried to help my kids find something to be happy about.

When the holidays came, we focused on giving thanks. My brother John and his wife, Eileen, hosted our Thanksgiving. We played games, visited and ate a lot! His wife, Eileen was a good cook and it was evident that she enjoyed being so hospitable.

For that one day, we pushed back the concern of the next treatment and gave thanks for what we had. Thanksgiving also gave us a renewed hope. Christmas would mark the end of the chemo treatments.

Time seemed to pass quickly between the Thanksgiving and Christmas holidays. I remember looking out my window and remembering how much joy I received by just walking in the fresh snow. It brought a memory of walking in the snow with beautiful snowflakes falling from the sky. I would hold my head back and catch the flakes upon my tongue. The flakes were so beautiful in the sun; it was as if each one was a brilliant diamond.

I remember watching my children play in the snow and felt warm tears run down my face. I was both thankful for the memory and hopeful that I would be present for Christmases to come. I was thirty-five-years-old, and couldn't even throw a snowball without assistance. I was so very weak and weary. Looking back, it seems like such a conundrum to be both strong and weak at the same time, but I think I was. I had to have been.

I had one more trip to the dingy hospital where they would do all the tests. We drove away from the farm on bald tires feeling hopeful. This was the final treatment. Maybe this would be the trip that put me into remission. The last time, I wasn't even sad as we drove to Minneapolis. We checked out the fence, and it still wasn't finished. We laughed as we drove by the house where we were tempted to stop and eat their picnic. We didn't dare speak it, but we were both so very hopeful that this would be my last trip for chemotherapy.

Jim dropped me off at the alley door next to the same pile of used hospital equipment, like always. I waited for him to park, and we walked down the familiar halls together and greeted the nurse who had become our friend.

We rode the elevator, and Jim flashed his box of Dots at the nurses as we checked on our friends.

The nurses didn't disappoint and had reserved the television and Jim's bed.

I was taken down for my last peachy chalky drink, which I gagged on, reminding myself that this was my LAST chalky peach drink! I endured through more CAT scans and MRIs. The entire time I prayed.

## THE SHADOW SCARE

I was devastated when my doctor explained to me that they had seen a shadow on the scans. He explained that the next step was exploratory surgery, and of course, it needed to be done immediately.

I was so angry! Didn't he know that I was to be done with these horrible treatments? Didn't he care that I had plans to spend Christmas with my family? As always, Jim's calming presence helped me to come back to reality, place my feet firmly on the floor and prepare for the next battle.

The doctor explained that the next step would be a new, nuclear medicine study. Antibodies would be drawn from my blood, and charged, whatever that meant. Then, the antibodies would be put back into the bloodstream. The hope was that the charged antibodies would be drawn to the cancer cells and would light up in the exact location of the cancer.

Jim and I were not completely sure about the details of what was explained, but we had learned to trust his judgment and had full confidence in his plan. I gave the doctor permission to begin the nuclear medicine study and reminded him that I wanted to be home to celebrate Christmas with my family. He promised nothing, but said he would do what he could.

The blood work was done right away, but the nuclear medicine procedure was to begin the next day. Very early the next morning, we walked down the long dark hallway and were ushered into a room that had dark heavy covering over the window and was taped on all sides so light couldn't enter. Even the side door had been taped shut. I was immediately fearful.

Although the doctor's had explained to me that I would need to be contained in a dark room for 24 hours, actually spending the time in the room brought much anxiety. Jim felt my fear and requested that he stay with me for the twenty-four hours. I was, once again, reminded how lucky I was to have such a man. The nurses explained that we would be in the room alone and we must remain in the dark environment for 24 hours.

Jim didn't even hesitate. He would stay and help me through yet another difficult treatment. The nurses set the IV dripping and left us alone. Theytaped the outside door we were left to wait. Four hours into the test, the door was opened we were informed that the test would not work on me.

I was frustrated and confused, but the doctor came back with a new, old plan – surgery. Although I wasn't eager for another round, I just wanted it over. I reminded him that I wanted to be home by Christmas. Again, no promises were made.

As I was prepped for surgery, I was informed of all the possibilities. When I was finally wheeled into surgery, I was sick at heart and depressed. I remember thinking about how odd life could be. It had been just a day or so earlier that I had been over the moon happy.

I came out of surgery to Jim giving me a thumbs up. The surgery had gone well, and the shadow was only my ovaries. Once again, our hopes escalated! It was five days until Christmas. I had tubes shooting out everywhere, but I was determined that I would be home for Christmas!

Biopsies were sent to the lab, and I was taken up to my little hospital room to recover. It took that surgery for me to realize that the cancer wing had much nicer rooms than the surgery wing. I wanted to go home so very badly!

I had planned on one last easy trip and I was struggling to accept the changes that were taking place. I knew the surgery had gone well. The doctor had moved and checked every part of my stomach, but they wanted to be thorough!

## OPTIONS!

Two days before Christmas, the doctors came into my room to share the biopsy results. Before they even spoke, we knew the report was not good. The tests found cancer cells in my liver and bone marrow. The chemotherapy had not killed all the cancer cells.

Before I even had a chance to digest this new and horrific finding, the doctors began giving me my treatment choices. According to them, I had three choices: do nothing and live for six months, complete another round of chemotherapy and live maybe a year, or have a bone marrow transplant, and if all the cancer cells were killed, I would be cured. I didn't even want to think about what happened if the cancer cells were not killed.

I was so shocked that I couldn't even think. I came for my last treatment, feeling stronger and better and certain that the cancer was gone. Now I was informed that not only did I still have cancer, but I needed to start all over with treatment!

We thought only briefly before we decided to go with option number three:, bone marrow transplant. The technical term, Autologous Bone Marrow transplant, was still experimental. Our insurance was good, but the procedure would cost $175,000 and no insurance covered an experimental treatment. The treatment could be done, if the insurance would pay the hospital. I knew the doctors were willing to do their part, and if the insurance company would agree to payment, I would surely do mine.

The doctor explained that there were a few other funding options. The University Hospital had some grant money that may pay a portion, but my age was against me. The doctor would write the insurance company, but warned me to not get my hopes up.

If money for the transplant were secured, doctors would use my own bone marrow to replace the cancer cells in my body. The rejection rate or a transplant using my own bone marrow would be much less than if I used a sibling's bone marrow. But it was a matter of money.

## BONE MARROW TRANSPLANT

There was nothing I could do to speed up the process of the pending bone marrow transplant, so I focused my efforts on making it home for Christmas. On Christmas Eve, the surgeon came into my room for a post-op check. I had tubes everywhere and was extremely weak, but I told him that I wanted, needed to be home for Christmas.

I was told that once my stomach began working, I could leave the hospital. I told that surgeon that I had given three treatment options to think about and the first two offered death. The third option gave me a chance of remission, but no one could guarantee me life. No one could guarantee that I would be home for Christmas the next year, and I would spend this Christmas, the only one I was guaranteed, with my children.

I was as shocked as anyone when he reached over and took the tubes out of my nose and told the doctors that I was to be released to go home. I was never so happy to be leaving.

With the news of my homecoming, my brother and sister-in-law, John and Eileen, brought Christmas dinner to our home and all my family was there. Jim and I didn't arrive until 6:00 p.m. Christmas Eve, and the yard was full of cars. People came from everywhere, even some I didn't expect.

The kids' Sunday school program was to be held that evening and I insisted on going. The program had already started when Jim wheeled me into the church. I knew that I looked like death warmed over. I had no makeup on and wore a scarf over my head. There were over fifty staples in my stomach, and I was completely and totally exhausted, but I would not miss what could, quite possibly, have been the last Christmas program I would see.

After the program, we had our traditional Christmas feast. There was oyster stew and milk dumplings and all the traditional favorites, but I couldn't eat any of it! I didn't even care. I was so very thankful to be home, and at that moment, nothing else was more important. Later, we opened our Christmas gifts, received two special gifts, a set of pretty towels and a small, colored television that we couldn't afford, but Jim wanted me to have when we were at the hospital.

The entire family was there for Christmas. Some slept at Mom's and others stayed with Jim's parents. Kids were lying all over. It was great! This truly was an old fashioned Christmas, but what was not said was how desperately sick I was.

Paula caught me crying and realized how sad I was. Jim explained to her that I was really sick, and she should just spend time with me.

Although most of that treasured Christmas was the exact therapy I needed, but there was a dark cloud that still makes me sad. Jim's brother had been taking care of the farm chores when we were in Minneapolis, something for which we were immensely thankful.

I walked in on a conversation that I wished I had never heard and still hurts me today. My sister-in-law was upset, and I overheard a conversation about me that was very hurtful. Jim's dad saw my face and asked what happened as I went back to my house, needing to be alone. I understood that family members were tired of my sickness. I knew my sister-in-law had never liked the farm, and now, because of my cancer, she and my brother-in-law were saddled with the milking and chores, and she had a family and job to maintain. I did understand her feelings, but I was so hurt. Did she think that cancer treatments were a choice I'd made? Didn't she know that if the tables were turned that I would've cared for her family? It hurt my heart more than anything. What we were all going through was more than enough! We had a heavy enough load without any cruel remarks.

On New Year's Day, we received a telephone call from the University Hospital. The doctor was excited to report that the insurance company had agreed to pay for the bone marrow transplant. It was the best news.

Of course, I was ecstatic to be offered another chance, but I knew that it would be the last. I was still very concerned about the state of our farm. My sister-in-law's words still rang in my ears. But I had to try the treatment.

My father-in-law assured me that the farm would be taken care of, and he was a man of his word. I was told to report to University Hospital the next day. We packed our bags once again, hugged and kissed my precious children, and prayed that this would not be the last time I spent with my beloved family.

We left home that New Year's Day hoping and praying that the decision we made was right. Fear had risen to new and greater heights. I had no assurances that the bone marrow transplant would even work, but I knew that without it, my life would most certainly be cut short.

My inner spirit told me to fear not! And I tried, but the devil worked overtime, and my fears were his playground.

This time, leaving home was different. I think we are all certain that this was THE last ditch effort. If this treatment didn't work, I would die. I didn't feel that I had any choice, though. Transplant was the only option that offered the chance to a long life. So I kept repeating the mantra. "Barb, put your feet down. It's time to be strong."

We entered the hospital with my new television in hand and a knowledge that this treatment would make all the rest look mild. I had to be prepared for the ultimate battle, and with strength and hope and prayer, I would win.

Due to the holiday schedule, I was told that the doctor's would work quick because the surgery schedule was slower during that time.

The anesthesiologist was scheduled to come that evening and explain the pending procedure, but he didn't. The medical staff spent much time telling me not to worry and assuring me that they knew what they were doing.

WRONG!

The doctor overslept and didn't arrive until 5:00 a.m. My potassium levels, which should've been checked pre-op, were low. I had to be given two units of potassium before they even could start the surgery. When the surgeon came in to explain the procedure, he asked when the anesthesiologist had visited me. I told him that he had come at 5:00 a.m. With that the gloves came off, followed by the scrubs. Because the anesthesiologist was late, thesurgery schedule was thrown off and would need to be postponed. Later, the doctor told me that if I had had the surgery with my potassium being so low, I would have died. Had the pre-op been done the night before, as he requested, everything could have gone according to schedule, but it didn't.

January 1985 was beginning to be already a pretty bad year! First, I had to leave my family and come to the University Hospital again, and the surgery was botched. I prayed things would get better soon.

The surgery was rescheduled for January 3, 1985, and it was to take place in the emergency surgery room. They used a different method of anesthesiology, the only time I had ever been sick from anesthesia.

The surgery lasted five hours. The doctor drilled into my hip bones and inserted a needle that was used to draw out the bone marrow, 1/2 teaspoon at a time. I was punctured between eighty and ninety times so they could acquire enough bone marrow.

Jim was alone throughout the five hour surgery and the five hours felt like an eternity. In surgery, the doctors cleansed my bone marrow of cancer cells, froze it and kept it in a lab for the future transplant. Tests were run on me to ensure that I did not have an infection.

Once the anesthetic wore off, my legs hurt so badly. I knew I could withstand a lot of pain, but that was almost unbearable. Jim spent the day rubbing the soreness in my legs. They continued to hurt for days after that surgery. The nurse cleaned and checked my teeth and ears for infection. They inserted a Hickman catheter.

On January 13, I was moved into ICU and an IV was started. The IV would run for twenty-four hours and its purpose was to kill off my entire immune system, including the cancer cells.

## D DAY

By this time in our marriage and throughout my entire cancer treatment, I was certain that Jim loved me. His loyalty and perseverance in the "in sickness" clause of our vows had been thoroughly tested, and he passed with flying colors. Still, I was moved to tears more than once when I watched my beloved Jim sleep on the floor with just a pillow the entire seven days I was in intensive care. My doctor had given him permission to stay with me in ICU and that was unheard of. I think he realized that this was a battle we were fighting as a team, and I needed him with me.

While in ICU, it wasn't possible to call and speak with the kids because there wasn't a telephone. I was lonely and missed them. The emptiness in my heart was always fresh and painful. It seems that with all the absence and treatment I had been though, being away would be easier. It never was.

Jim watched everything that was being done to me. By this time in my treatments, Jim had learned to be trusting of the doctors, but watchful. He would look out for my well-being at all costs. January 14 was my scheduled D-day, or should I say C-day. The doctors were to administer three different types of chemotherapy drugs at the same time. The combination was five times stronger than what I'd had before.

Every doctor and nurse watched as my heart rate rose. We all feared that this could be the end. I knew I could have a heart attack at any time. The doctor told me they couldn't stop the therapy for any reason, even cardiac failure. My heart continued to climb, reached a peak, plateaued for a time, and then slowly began to lower. The chemotherapy drugs made my skin feel and look as if I'd been sunburned. The doctors called it French chemotherapy and told me that it would cleanse my liver of cancer cells.

As the doctor's had expected, I had diarrhea and a lot of vomiting. I was so sick throughout that I prayed for an end, no matter what that might be. My body burned a bright red, sores formed on my lips and inside my mouth. I was so medicated that I struggled to maintain consciousness, and when I was awake, I was vomiting or experiencing uncontrollable diarrhea. The process took six consecutive days. It was the worst hell I could remember living through. After the six days of treatment I would be given two days of rest. Rest! Who did they think they were kidding? There is no rest during this process.

The doctors and nurses could count on me staying upbeat, but the bone marrow process was almost more than I could bear. My every action was monitored closely. I couldn't brush my teeth for fear of cutting my gums. Any little cut and I could bleed to death.

During the limbo between the chemotherapy and the transplant, doctors from all over the world stood by my hospital bed. They monitored everything and explained that the bone marrow would find its way back to the bone marrow, and with success, new and cancer-free bone marrow would begin to regenerate.

Once I was ready, we were moved from ICU back to the isolation room where Jim finally had his cot and pillow. He would stay in my room, but because my immune system was compromised, would be limited in his coming and going.

We started a brand new "be careful" program. Because I was extremely weak and had absolutely no red cells, white cells, or platelets, I was at risk with everything I did. Without platelets, I could bleed to death with the tiniest cut. For thirteen days, I had less than fifty white blood cells in my entire body. The doctors told us that one must have at least 50 cells in order to be counted. They explained that white blood cells were my infection fighters and I only had 50. A normal, healthy person has around 5-10 thousand. It wasn't until the fourteenth day that they were able to count 50 cells.

Every day, I was given two bags of red cells, two bags of platelets, and five different antibiotics. They became my immune system. My IV ran twenty four hours a day to keep me alive. Jim went out to eat once a day and before returning to our room, he had to wash with a special soap on his hands and arms to rid him of the bacteria he may have come into contact with when he was out. I learned a lot about bacteria during that time. I couldn't eat lettuce or pepper or keep any plants or flowers in my room due to the high likelihood of them containing bacteria.

Most days were filled with watching television and playing cards, and we both always looked forward to receiving mail. My sister, Madonna, wrote everyday, and I treasured her words. Because of my frail state, I wasn't allowed to be around people as I had before. I understood the need to be overly careful, but I wanted the isolation to end.

The doctors and nurses were forthright when explaining the next steps to all the different treatments I had endured, but all the words in the dictionary could not have prepared me for the actual bone marrow transplant.

Once the process began, my entire body seemed to turn inside and out. Everything about me changed, right down to the smell of my breath. My lungs gave off the most rancid smell and naturally, it came out in my breath. My skin hurt to touch, the inside of my mouth was covered in sores.

But, no matter how bad my breath smelled, Jim always had a loving goodnight kiss and was unwavering in his strength, constantly assuring me that we would make it through. Jim never complained and was with me everyday. He played cards and watched more television in the hospital than in all the rest of his life.

With every passing day, we became more aware of what "experimental" really meant. No one could possibly fathom what was happening to my body without experiencing it themselves. With every new procedure, there was always another release form for me to sign.

We just continued to pray that God would make it work.

## ONE ANTIBIOTIC TO TRY

We recognized everyone in the cancer ward. Some I felt empathy for and others were cold and full of self-pity. They literally were unable to communicate. For those people, I felt much sympathy.

I remember a twelve-year-old boy who went through his bone marrow transplant the week before mine. His parents catered to his every whim—just as we would have it had been one of our children lying on that bed.

The doctors had allowed him to leave his room and mingle with others. He played bingo, and Jim had even seen him eating lunch in the cafeteria. Jim and I were cautiously happy for him and even commented on the resiliency of youth.

On his thirteenth birthday, his parents hired a clown to dance and sing in celebration. The entire ward heard about the party and were invited to attend, but we listened through the wall and imagined the rest.

It wasn't long after his birthday party that he caught a virus and was quickly moved into isolation. It happened so quickly. We heard that his father was being paged and later on, we learned this barely, thirteen-year-old child had died.

Each death brought a new sadness to our hearts, but his was a harsh reality check. If a twelve-year-old boy could not fight this stuff, how could I? And would I be next?

Why would God take a young boy who had not even tasted the gift of life? It took a long time and lots of coaxing and support from the doctors, nurses and Jim to get my head together again before I began to think positively.

There were so many others who, like me, were faced with devastating circumstances. I remember a woman approximately my age whom I couldn't help but think that we may have been friends, if not for the cancer that left each of us in our rooms, isolated. She had leukemia and was working diligently with the doctors, unsuccessfully, to push her disease into remission. Following chemotherapy treatment, her cell count wouldn't come up. She, like me, had been hopeful. She wanted to go home and see her children, but was told that the treatment was unsuccessful. Unlike me, she was forced to do the majority of her fighting all alone. Her husband was unable to be with her during the darkest times. He flew in once a month and was able to stay with her only a few hours on the weekend before he had to leave. She had been there seven months—basically alone.

I remember seeing her one morning when I was out doing my daily, early morning walk. I chose early mornings for my walk because there were fewer people to see me, covered with a mask and scarf walking the halls. Most days, I was too weak to care about appearance, but on the occasion that I did think about my looks, I felt plain and ugly.

That morning, as I walked by the door of the lady with leukemia, I heard her say that she had had enough. She soon left to go home and be with her children. I never saw her again.

Each death affected me tremendously and would bring depression and great sadness. But I had to keep looking forward. I often think about that time and wonder why I wasn't chosen for death. I have never found an answer to that question, is it to be here for my children, my husband, or my mother. Maybe one day the answer will be given.

That time during the transplant was hard! We tried to put on a good front for the kids, but with each phone call came a harsh and abrupt loniness.

I was one month post transplant, and had learned the new language of bone marrow transplant quite well. Everything was charted and monitored. We were diligent about following the rules. Dr. Jim continued to be my protector and medial advisor, quizzing everyone who entered to ensure my safety.

Even with our diligence, I still contracted an infection. The doctor's felt that the five antibiotics that I was already taking were not enough to fight the infection, but there was one option they felt might help. The doctor cam in and said the words, “Barb, there is one more antibiotic we can try to beat this infection, if it doesn't work then you will die.” The undeniable truth hit me like a brick wall.

After that, I was fairly certain that I was going to die. Everybody I knew in the hospital isolation floor, that got an infection died. I was scared! I wasn't going to die from cancer but an infection? An infection is what killed that twelve-year-old boy! What chance would I have to survive? My spirit hit rock bottom, my fight had been fought, and I was tired. I was ready to give up.

Jim was there to keep me strong. I was so weak, I could barely lift my hands. Was it my time? Not knowing what else to do, Jim did the only thing he could think of. He pulled me into his temporary bed that was parked next to mine, and he held me close. I know he didn't sleep a wink, that night, but I slept like a baby in the arms of my faithful and loving husband.

The new antibiotic was scheduled to be administered in the late part of the evening when the nursing staff wasn't as busy. The doctor's warned us again about the side effects, but there really wasn't an option. This was the only antibiotic they felt would successfully fight off the infection that could kill me.

The start of the antibiotic was rather uneventful, but soon after the drug entered my system, it was evident that the side effects had started. I began to shake uncontrollably and my body temperature began rising. I shook so badly that the nurse administered medication to help with the shaking, the first one only slowing the shaking, and the second to provide me with some rest. My temperature reached a dangerous peak of 105 degrees. The experience, like so many others before it, pushed me to even greater peaks of pain. But I survived.

At 4:00 a.m., I woke up dripping in sweat after the fever broke. The second administration of the medicine had allowed me to rest, so during some of the most hairy times that evening, I slept. Jim recalls that night as being extremely frightening. He said that it was almost instantly that the side effects began. My body shook so violently it was like I was having a seizure. My teeth chattered so much the nurses feared I may bite off my tongue. I vaguely remember when both the nurse and Jim climbed into my tiny hospital bed in an attempt to warm me and calm my shaking body.

The first treatment was just a warm up. The antibiotic was to be administered each night at 10 p.m. for 20 days in a row, possibly longer. Another harsh lesson I learned while fighting cancer is that nothing is done singularly. Treatments are done in batches, and the side effects hit hard after each administration.

The next 20 days were rough. The drug was administered, the shaking began. Jim and the nurse would crawl into bed and attempt to keep me warm during the worst of it. Medication was administered to calm the shakes, and eventually a second and third administration were necessary to provide me with a little more relief and finally rest. I don't know how I would've survived without all of the prayers that were sent up in my name.

## MICHELLE'S BIRTHDAY

One of my nurses was a minister's wife, and she would often join Jim and me in our verbal therapy. She asked daily if people were praying for me, and then, read the Bible from the book of John. Her presence brought such a calming, love to my little isolation room. With her constant prayer and support, I began to force myself to begin to think positively.

Pray—pray without ceasing and then, pray again! Get your family involved and be included in prayer chains. Madonna called daily and prayed with me. Her telephone bill must have been horrendous, but she never complained. Jim had to hold the telephone for me during her calls. I wasn't strong enough to even do that. I know they carried me through the darkest times and back into yearning for life!

Obviously, we were unable to leave the hospital during this entire ordeal, and we both needed something to get us looking forward. Michelle, our youngest, would celebrate her 13th birthday in February, the kids were coming to the University for a visit. That was what I focused on during those difficult moments, seeing our beloved family.

Before calling home, we spoke with the doctors to gain permission for their visit. I asked to be allowed to decorate my room with birthday decorations for the party. I always made the kids birthdays special and I wanted to continue the tradition as best I could. We knew that everyone would need to be masked and gowned, but we didn't care. The presence of our family made everything worthwhile.

I expended most of my energy making a happy birthday banner for Michelle and hanging it in the window of my little room with a few balloons. Michelle asked for a basketball for her birthday, and Jim and I decided she would get one. Jim walked miles to get that basketball, but wouldn't stop until he found one.

Kelly, who had just received his drivers license, would drive the crew into Minneapolis. City driving was seriously different than the country roads of SD, but the crew arrived safely. I can't even describe how emotional I was when my family, my reason for fighting cancer, came into my room that day. The kids looked like angels clothed in masks, gloves and gowns They, of course, found the get-up silly and giggled in their costumes. We hugged, kissed, giggled and cried, and then started the routine all over again until there were no more tears to shed. What a difference it was to shed tears of joy!

The only difficult spot of that visit was my mother. She acted uptight and jealous, irritated that I had greeted my children first instead of her. She cranked about me giving the kids my leftover food, which in her mind I should have eaten myself, adding that those kids didn't need that food and that they were eating well all the time. Her rant, although I'm sure fueled by worry and anxiety, made the visit difficult, but we all tried to ignore her outbursts.

The kids were busting at the seams and wanted to tell us everything that was going on, but Mom continually interrupted. I think she wanted me all to herself, but I just needed to be with my kids. I tried, but it was so very difficult to act like everything was going well.

The toughest time during that initial visit was after Jim ordered pizza. As with most foods, I took one bite and had to lunge for my bucket? This upset Mom, and after a few minutes, her tirade upset Jim so much that he walked out of the room without saying anything to me. I knew he was upset, and felt like my lifeline had walked out.

Mom felt badly that Jim had left and said it was her fault. She was right, but what could I say. All I wanted was to spend a joyous time with my family. Why did there need to be conflict?

The visit was already tainted with the effects of cancer, silly, petty conflict within the family wouldn't make the visit better. I had no hair and was forced to wear a dumb scarf, my face was puffy from medication, and I vomited with every food combination just looking at food. And yet, I tried desperately to pretend like I was on top of the world looking down.

Throughout the visit, I tried to ignore my mother's antics, but the girls wanted to know why she was trying to upset me. Jim did return, and we eventually made it through the visit, but it was tense and exhausting. By the time everyone left for the motel, I could barely stay awake. The visit was bittersweet and even with the conflicts, I wanted nothing more than to keep my family with me. I knew that the next day would be tough when I was forced to say goodbye again.

## ANTIBIOTIC IS WORKING

The antibiotic routine continued for three weeks, and praise the Lord, it began to work. Small victories were the only ones I had at that point in time. Joy was rare on the cancer ward, but the nursing staff and patients did the best we could to find something to cling to during that time. Cancer was always in the forefront on our ward, and there was little outside entertainment, but we tried to make the best of it.

With the antibiotic treatments, I had no appetite. No one could convince me to eat, but pushed me to try something, anything. But every time I tried something, I made a mad dash for my bucket. If I had a hankering for a Whopper, Jim would make the walk to BK and bring it back. One bite, and I reached for my barf bucket again.

On the ward, Jim was known as the Candy Man. Anytime he left the ward, he would return with a sweet treat that he knew I liked. When Jim returned with his treats, they would threaten to wrestle him for the candy.

One nurse had Jim doing pushups and situps because he was sitting in the hospital all day. Jim was always good-natured, and responded to the nurse, pregnant at the time, "Who's getting fat?"

Those little gestures of kindness and humor are the gems that kept us looking forward. Words can't aptly describe the roller coaster ride of our emotions. With each nugget of humor we were met with doubts and questions and hurdles and pain, not to mention the seemingly never-ending stay on the ward.

How does one stay positive?

Jim and I did our best to look forward. We focused on the cards we received from friends and our treasured Sunday calls to the kids. But when I spoke with the kids, I searched for even one positive thing I could tell them. The best I could muster was a litany of nice cards I'd received that week. How boring for a kid to hear about!

To keep our minds busy, we would often talk about all the people that we had met in the hospital. We had met so many incredible people on our long journey. I had made one particularly good friend during my long chemotherapy treatment. I remember lying in the same bed during our treatments visiting with one another while our husbands left to eat dinner together.

Marty took a picture of us taking our chemotherapy together. When I saw the picture, I almost died! I remember laughing and joking that I looked like I was already dead. But Marty told me that he hung that picture on his register at work. Marty took his wife home after the chemo treatments, and like so many others that we met on the ward, she passed away a year later. My heart was broke for her family.

Many of the people we reminisced about were due to some of my most embarrassing moments. I remembered a very handsome, young orderly who picked me up before the Hickman catheter surgery. I assured him that I could walk to the gurney and as I swung my arm, I caught my hospital gown and flipped the thing right over his head, giving him quite a show.

With the treatments I had endured, all strength left my body. The doctors told me that I had to build my strength by walking. And so we walked and talked. No matter how horrible I felt, we walked. I needed strength to go home, so I pushed forward.

The walks were short. I could manage 10-15 minutes before collapsing from exhaustion in my bed. But the doctors kept pushing for more, and Jim and I would go again. I pushed myself until I was so tired that I wasn't sure I could make it back to bed.

My upper body strength needed to be built up again as well For that, I began crafting dogs out of yarn. For each dog I wrapped the yarn 100 times around a piece of cardboard. Not only did I have to work my arms, but I had to count. The crafting reminded me of how I used to work my upper body when I did crafts at home or baked bread or raked the lawn. I doubt the girls ever understand the sweat and tears that went into those yarn dogs. For Kelly, I made a leather loop belt. All of these projects were meant to help me regain strength in my entire body. I remember getting a beautiful lap quilt from a church group during that time too. I was honored to receive the blanket and was told to use it to keep myself warm, but it was far too pretty to be used as a foot cover. I gave it to Jim and told him that I would save it so that I could give it to our first grandchild. That memory sticks with me as one where my positivity returned. I was thinking about grandchildren, and that meant I would not only survive this disease, but conquer.

## STAIRS LIKE MT EVEREST

As I slowly regained strength, thinking about the future and going home was something that I was ready to discuss. The new challenge was maintaining 1000 cells WBC (white blood count) and ability to climb a flight of stairs. Those stairs looked a lot like Mount Everest to me, but I was determined to not be defeated! I am going to go home!

I had been becoming more active without really thinking about it, but there was a lot of work to be done. I continued my walks through the cancer ward and my crafting to keep my arms and mind active. I looked out into the sunshine at the college students and dreamed of the day that I would once again walk in the same sunshine.

My effort in gaining physical strength was often countered with obstacles. Once again, I had to steel myself for the loss of one of my cancer friends. This time, the friend was 21, beautiful, and a new mom. Chemotherapy for the leukemia diagnosis took her beautiful hair and her spirit.

Another friend, one who had given me a guardian angel pin to boost my spirits lost her life to cancer in just one short year. I still think of her each time that I look at the angel pin.

Each time a cancer friend left this earth, my heart ached for their family. Each time a cancer friend left this earth, I contemplated my own life and possible death. More than anything, I learned that life and death is not something we control. It is God who decides and once again the question "Why wasn't I chosen for death?"

## HISTORY REPEATS

For three months, I did everything I was instructed to do. I walked, I climbed the stairs, and I did therapy. I took every test and aced them all. What more could they want or need? Of course, in the hospital, there were always more tests, and that is what they needed.

The doctors knew that I had regained my strength, I could carry on a conversation and loved having company. Because of my progress, I was given the privilege of leaving the hospital, so one weekend, some family friends came and brought our children. We had dinner out—not a bland hospital tray, but real food!

I ordered a plain omelet with no onions. Of course, as soon as I was able to, and was hungry for some real food, the blasted restaurant screwed up my order and brought me an omelet with onions. Three orders later, the waitress brought yet another onion-laden omelet. I was so annoyed! Finally a decent meal and it was spoiled with onions. I packed up my twelve pieces of toast and we left.

Our children were wonderful during the trip to Minneapolis. My friend reported that they were kind, polite and helpful. There were no kid arguments or bickering. We were proud of them!

Soon after that visit, my doctor came in and said, "The bone marrow came back negative." which meant there were no cancer cells in my marrow. I was never so excited! With those results, a WBC count of 1000, and me walking up the flight of stairs, the doctor FINALLY asked me if I'd like to go home.

My response was, "I am out of here—where do I sign!"

Until the moment arrived, I hadn't allowed myself to think about going home before because I feared it would never happen. Now a month earlier than was anticipated, we were going home! Wow—thank you, God! The bone marrow test was the one cloud that continued to hang over my head, but the results would come in soon and with the continued grace of God,

my marrow was clear.
And, history repeated itself. Or, at least, God provided for us again. When Jim got ready to retrieve our car, which had been parked in the same lot that charged by the day, he emptied his pockets and we counted every penny and piece of lint.

Together, we had a hundred dollars left, and no matter how you counted it, it would not have been enough to pay the parking fee. The cost to get our car out should have been $305. But, Jim returned to get me with a grin from ear to ear. Although we had been parked in that lot from January 1 to April 2, the attendant charged $5 for the stay.

## THE LORD TOUCHED ME

On our homecoming, the kids made a new welcome home banner, my mother cleaned the carpets, and the neighbors brought bags of groceries again. That says so much about the generosity of my family and friends. I loved them all dearly.

Everyone was overjoyed with our early homecoming, but the doctor would be calling with the results of my bone marrow test. He said it would take three days, and those were the longest three days ever. I tried to be positive, but that lingering fear of bad news never left me.

Madonna, my fervently prayerful sister, was with me when the call came. I had her answer the call and begged her to keep the news from me if the cancer was back. Thankfully, joyfully, there was no need to lie. The bone marrow was clear. We spent the rest of that day and many others celebrating and thanking God for His mercy and grace.

The news was great, but I still had a long journey to be well and healthy. My orders were to rest and stay stress free. Others were to do the housework and I was to rest and recover.

I was screened for any viruses, and friends didn't seem to mind when they were told that if they were ill not to visit. I made twice weekly trips to Aberdeen for blood work.

The kids were my greatest help! The girls cooked and cleaned. Kelly helped with the chores. He continued to earn fifteen dollars a month for his work, and continued to supply money for the girls when they needed it, unbeknownst to us.

Jim bought me a little red toy Pomeranian puppy to keep me company. That puppy was just what I needed to keep me occupied during my days of recovery, especially since Jim had returned home to the chores and spring planting.

I won tickets for a June performance of Boxcar Willie, and Jim and I made that our first night out. It felt so incredibly good to just be a normal, married couple. I'd almost forgotten how much fun we had together. But, those bills. Wow, did they pile up! We received 17 separate bills every single month. They were from hospitals, doctors and clinics. And, once again, the bill collectors started calling. I found it humorous how each collector provided me with a suggestion for how we could pay their particular bill, and of course, theirs was the most important.

I did what I could and paid a little every month on every bill. I didn't play favorites; each one was paid something, and I knew that someday we would make it to the end.

I stayed home almost all the time, but in my weakened state, I still fought pneumonia 4-5 times that first year. I was so weak and feared that the cancer would come back. Depression set in no matter how hard I tried to stay positive.

I could leave the house to do errands, but I wasn't able to carry the bags myself. On one particular day, I stopped at our local grocery store to get a few things. I knelt down to get an item on the bottom rack, and once I got down, I was too weak to get back up.. I crawled on my hands and knees to the cooler case and used it for support to help me stand. Even with my walking and crafting, I was weaker than I had ever realized. I knew I was falling deeper into depression, but I didn't know how to get out.

Following cancer treatment many will fall into depression. My life had been consumed with doctors and hospitals for the past year. One would think I would be happy and excited because I was past the worst of times, but it wasn't like that. I could no longer work at the job I truly loved, I was so weak that I rarely left the couch in my living room, and it seemed everyone's life around me moved forward but mine stood still. I lived in a state of constant worry; Would the cancer come back? Would I ever regain my strength? What will be my next hurdle?

God knew what I needed, He always seemed to provide for me at my most difficult times. He was there during my numbness in my legs, when I needed strength to return home, when I needed the insurance company to provide for the bone marrow transplant, and even when we didn't have enough money to pay the parking fees. I knew He was always guiding me on the long journey, but this day was different.

An acquaintance from church showed up at my home, I would see her in church on Sunday morning and we would smile at each other and say "Hi" but I only knew her as a lady from church. When she arrived at my home, she asked if I would be willing to allow her to pray for me. It really wasn't a strange request but when she said, "I have had this feeling that I need to come and put my hands on you and pray." I thought it was a little unusual. However, I would never turn away anyone that was willing to pray with me. I needed every ounce of prayer anyone was willing to give. She sat next to me on what became my resting place each day- the living room couch. I folded my hands across my lap and closed my eyes, she placed her hand on mine and began to pray. The words flowed out of her like a beautiful hymn and I began to feel a comforting warmth that started at my feet and moved slowly to the top of my head. The prayer continued but I no longer heard any words, I saw an angelic bright light at my feet. The light was so breath taking and calming,. Within the glow of the light stood a shadow of a man. When she finished her prayer, which seemed to be only a few minutes, I felt peaceful, the most peaceful calm that I had ever felt in my life. When she got up to leave we realized she had been there praying for over an hour. I know that day the Lord healed me of my battle with cancer.. I knew from this day forward my strength would come back. All those worries, were gone! All those questions, answered by the grace of God

Every three months, Jim and I returned to the University for my quarterly check up. The doctors would put me through the battery of tests; CAT scans, bone marrow, and blood work. We would wait 3 days for the results to come back. One might worry about the results and ask the question, "Is my cancer back?" But I had my answer, the Lord had given me peace.

## DO I HAVE AIDS?

After my clean bill of health, we rode the roller coaster of life, was doing well, until I received a letter from University Hospital. After I saw the letter, I just started crying. I couldn't even open it, fearing the worst. I bawled all the way to the barn and gave the letter to Jim.

The letter stated that I would need to come back to the University Hospital for blood tests. They said that I had received fifty pints of red blood and platelets that had never been tested for the HIV virus and I needed to be tested for AIDS. It was 1985, and the AIDS virus was scary and held all sorts of negative connotations. I couldn't tell anyone about the letter. I felt certain they would be too afraid to come to my place.

But, Dr. Jim returned with ease and he very calmly told me that everything would be alright. It took two months before the test results would come back. I tried my best to live the life I'd been blessed with, but once again, a black cloud hung over me.

A letter finally appeared in our mailbox. We opened the letter together, and even Jim's hands were shaking a little. But, the letter stated that I had been spared. I did NOT have AIDS!

I didn't have AIDS!

## CRUMBLED BACKBONE

In 1987, when I was to go back to University Hospital for my yearly check, I got so nervous. I knew I would need to complete the battery of tests again, but my back had been hurting badly. I knew something wasn't right, but the pain I was experiencing then wasn't like the first time. I tried to remind myself of the day the Lord healed me but worry would often find its way into my head.

I, of course, had consulted with Dr. H., the man who walked me through my entire treatment, and he scheduled me to a neurologist when I was at the hospital for the check up. His fear was that my backbone had crumbled and fallen forward. The amount of radiation to my back had not only destroyed the cancer but also weaken my bones. After the appointment with the neurologist, his suspicions were confirmed.

I wasn't even able to return home after the visit because tests showed that my spinal cord was being stretched so tightly it was ready to snap! The doctors wanted to put a halo crown on my head to keep me immobile, but I refused. I promised to lie still and follow their orders if they didn't put me in a halo. They agreed, and I did my part. We were once again in limbo, waiting for the back surgery to be scheduled.

To correct the stretched spinal cord, the doctors planned to break one of my ribs and fuse it in where my backbone had crumbled away. My back bone basically broken and I had shrunk four inches because of it.

The doctors attached sensors to my head, right on top of the head of hair that had finally grown back. They also attached sensors to my back. The sensors were their guide during the surgery to avoid important nerves that, if severed, would affect my life forever. The new bone was placed to straighten my bent body to an upright position.

Following the placement of the bone in my spine, the doctors waited only one week before performing a second surgery where they would put in steel rods, one on each side of my backbone. The rods ran from my shoulder blades to my tailbone. The rods were there to support until the fusion of the rib bone took hold. I was fitted with a body cast that took two days to build. The cast would provide my body a chance to heal from the two surgeries. I was anxious to go home and allow my tattered body to mend.

The summer heat made the brace very uncomfortable, but I could get around quite well with the brace, and I tried to not complain. Thankfully, I was able to remove the brace when sleeping. Being home with family and friends kept me functioning. Everyone needs a reason to get up, and they were mine. I got up every morning and put on the brace.

## CANCER OR STAPH INFECTION?

Fall and winter came quickly, and I was aware that the brace would make it more difficult for me to move on the ice and snow. However, I was thankful for the cooler weather.

With school beginning again, both our girls were busy with activities. Jim and I were so happy to be able to be a part of all their activities. We rarely missed home basketball games and tried to make many of the out-of-town games as well.

My girls' team, Groton, was scheduled to play Sisseton, the town where my brother lived, so we planned to attend the game and spend a few hours visiting with my brother and his wife.

The evening was great fun! We thoroughly enjoyed our visit and watching the girls cheer. We left the game, and the winter air was brisk, a light snow falling. We all were laughing, talking and walking. I unknowingly stepped on a snow-covered ice patch and my feet went out from under me. I fell to the ground before I even had a chance to stop myself. The brace dug into my bottom, and I lay flat on my back in the snow.

Everyone rushed around me, and I told them that I was ok. I wasn't even sure that I was hurt. I insisted that we keep our plans and go out for pizza. But, by the time we finished our meal, I knew something was wrong. By the time we drove the hour back to the farm, the pain in my back was intense.

I refused to go to the hospital. I refused to even talk about the hospital. Deep down, every single twinge I'd felt since I was declared to be in remission was something that created anxiety. I tried to pretend that the pain was improving. It wasn't. I prayed that I would heal myself, but I didn't.

I would wake up at night, my nightgown drenched in sweat, and immediately be carried back to cancer. Those were my first symptoms.

Finally after a few months of worry, I made an appointment in Aberdeen. It was April 1988, and the sun was shining. The doctors ordered a CAT scan and when they read the results they called Dr. H. immediately. Arrangements were made for us to leave right away to Minneapolis and back to the University Hospital. It was deja vu. Once again we made arrangements for the kids and asked Jim's brother to take care of the chores. We packed our suitcases and left the next morning, x-rays in hand.

The orthopedic doctor came in first, held the x-ray up to the sun-filled window, and felt certain that the cancer was back.

My heart sank to the depths of despair. All I could say was, "Oh no, oh no!"

My oncologist came in, looked at the same x-ray, and disagreed. We were more hopeful after the oncologist, disagreed, but the worry wouldn't end until they were certain.

Jim paced back and forth and wondering how he would tell the kids. The deep sadness in our hearts spilled over in our tears as we held each other.

The next morning, the orthopedic and oncologist had determined that surgery would need to be done to determine if the x-ray showed cancer or staph infection.

Jim called the family, and both our moms came along with John and Eileen to support Jim during the surgery. I was so thankful to have them come and be with him.

We were told that the surgery would take an hour if it were cancer. By the time I was wheeled into surgery, I was frantic and anxious. I was so upset that when the nurse saw me crying, she instructed the staff to get me to sleep. That was the last that I remembered.

When I woke up, I immediately asked for the time. If it was early in the day, I new it was cancer. If not, it was something else. I was so relieved when I was told it was 8:00 p.m., and I had been in surgery for hours. I found out later that they had been forced to remove my rods from my back because of staph infection.

The doctors opened my back at the spine and left an opening four inches deep and about two inches wide for the full length of my back. The incisions were to be left open for ten days, hopefully to rid my body of the infection. Every day the wounds were flushed and then bandaged up again. I received a morphine drip for the pain.

I was frustrated, I had my life to live and my eldest child was graduating in a few weeks. I didn't have time for this. But I didn't have a choice. Following the surgery I was determined to return in time for Kelly's graduation. When I prayed through my fight with cancer I often asked the Lord to allow me to see my children graduate from high school. If cancer didn't stop me, the surgery wasn't going to either.

I was allowed to leave in time for Kelly's graduation. They had to wheel me into the high school auditorium but I was there to celebrate. It was an emotional time for Kelly and me. Two years ago I wasn't certain I would see this day. There were many tears of joy, not only for Kelly's accomplishments but because I was able to witness it.

## EMERGENCY AMBULANCE

After the 10 days, I had to continue to take antibiotics for six weeks, but I could be home during that time. After the six weeks of antibiotics, I would need to have another surgery to replace the rods in my back.

I was thankful to be home, but still needed to complete the six week antibiotic regimen. The hospital made arrangements for Home Health Care to deliver the medication for each day's use, and Jim would administer the medications. Home Health Care rules required me to remain at home to receive their service. For the most part, that was not a problem.

After we'd been home approximately two weeks, our niece, Kim, was to be married. I had missed out on so many joyous occasions during my previous hospitalizations, and I wanted very much to attend her wedding. Jim didn't want to say no to me, and we both knew the consequences if we were caught.

The wedding was held in Sisseton, and we planned to spend the night. I had two IVs while there, but that didn't stop me. Our little excursion, unfortunately, was reported to Home Health, and because we'd broken the rules, they would no longer deliver the medications to our home. Instead, we would be forced to drive to Aberdeen twice a day for the IV.

I never did find out who reported me for leaving my house, but that report, and I guess my actions, sure changed the activity in our home. We drove fifty mile, twice daily, to get an IV, which took one and a half hours each time.

Jim couldn't break up his day to take me and I couldn't go alone, so Jim's mother agreed to take me. The twice a day routine was hard on both of us. I could tell that the trips were tiring her out, and one afternoon I suggested that she relax and I would have Jim take me for the second IV. She agreed.

The afternoon IV trip was fun with Jim. It broke up the monotony of the routine, and gave us a chance to visit. We hit Burger King for our favorite treats. When we started home, we passed an ambulance, lights flashing and speeding into town. I looked at Jim and told him that we knew who was in that ambulance. The hair on my arms stood up, and I hoped that my children were safe.

## JIM'S DAD

I repeated to Jim that we knew who was in that ambulance. Jim just ignored me and kept driving. But when we drove the last mile down our gravel road, and I think he finally believed me. Kelly met us, tears streaming down his cheeks, and told us that the ambulance held Grandpa, Jim's dad.

Kelly told us that he had stopped over to visit and noticed that his grandfather's color wasn't right. He started CPR and called for help. The ambulance came and took Jim's dad to the hospital and his wife, Meta, was able to ride with.

Jim's dad died on June 3 from a massive heart attack at Aberdeen hospital. Floyd and Meta had been able to eat one last dinner together. After dinner, Floyd told Meta that he wasn't feeling well and went to lie on the couch.

I believe God told me to tell Jim's mom to stay home that afternoon and have supper with her husband. I knew it was God who told me that we knew that person in the ambulance..

After that, life became really complicated. We had funeral arrangements to make and relatives coming. We needed to shop for groceries and all the rest that comes with the preparations for a funeral, and still, the chores needed to be done, and I still couldn't miss the trips to the Aberdeen hospital for the IV treatments.

## SURGERY

We made it through the funeral and through the remaining antibiotic treatments, and then it was time to redo my reconstructive back surgery. As always, Jim drove me to the hospital for the first surgery. Both our moms rode with us and stayed at a motel so that I would have support. After this surgery, Jim needed to return home to the farm. He wasn't able to stay with me as it was to difficult with Floyd being gone.

The surgery went well, and once again doctors removed a rib, this time from the other side. They even improved upon their technique, allowing blood to circulate through the bone, keeping it healthier.

We were forced to wait a week before the doctors could do the second surgery to replace the rods. I had had five major surgeries quite close together, and it had taken a toll on my body. After that surgery, the nurses could no longer find a vein for the blood transfusion. Their solution was to use my little finger, and it was successful. They pumped 23 pints of blood through it.

The surgery, to replace the steel rods, began about 10:00 a.m., and I remember being conscious and asking for Jim around midnight. Thankfully, the surgery had gone well and I was back in my room by 2:30 a.m.

Once I came to, I was in great pain. The head nurse had not been given the medication instructions by the doctor as he had been called away to an emergency surgery. She knew that I was in great pain, but could do nothing about it without the doctor's order. After what seemed like forever, the nurse took it upon herself to give me a morphine drip to lessen my suffering, even if it meant her job.

The doctor arrived later and apologized for not issuing the medication order sooner, and he made sure the charge nurse had orders for giving me pain medication without his order.

Jim again had to returned home and both our moms stayed to help me through the recovery. They got along great. Every day, they rode the motel shuttle bus back and forth to the hospital. It was good to see them laughing.

One day, they returned laughing really hard. Meta, Jim's mother, told the story with tears in her eyes with laughter. Meta walked through an open door to get on the shuttle bus, but my mother was busy gawking at a new married couple holding hands. When she turned she smacked into a pane of glass at full walking speed. She hit the glass so hard it bent her glasses. Embarrassed, she quickly got on the shuttle bus. Meta tried to hold back her laughter but when she looked at my mother, glasses still crooked on her face, they both busted out laughing. Of course, Meta reenacted the whole incident for my pleasure. They laughed for two days.

## RECUPERATING WITH BROKEN ARM

I was stuck in the hospital until I could regain strength, and once again, I would come home in a body cast. I was determined to do whatever the doctors told me, but my recovery from surgery was slow!

Slowly, I regained the use of my legs, but the dependence upon the brace combined with weak legs left me very insecure. I didn't have Jim's support during this surgery, so it was up to me to get myself focused and get back on my feet. I did what I needed to do and I made it home. It took me over a year to wean myself away from the back brace and support myself fully, but I kept working.

1989 was a year of transition and difficulty. Jim's mother moved out of the big farm house into an apartment in Groton. Jim and his brother, both of whom worked the family farm, were parting ways because our sister-in-law wanted to leave. They had been experiencing marital difficulties for awhile and were both ready for a change.

Their leaving the farm left Jim alone to milk 100 head of cows twice daily and farm four quarters of land. He was a slave to the land! Additionally, Jim assumed all the debt accrued by the farm to repay his brother for all the help we had received from him during my cancer treatments. On top of that, we were still paying our own debt from the past years of medical expenses. Jim worked long hours, sometimes more than 80 hours per week. I was often left alone to fend for myself, and because I'd had Jim by my side for the majority of my treatments, I missed our time together. I tried to stay busy the best I could.

Paula, our middle daughter, was also graduating in the spring of 1989. I was thrilled to be the one to make the party arrangements. I made a huge roaster of scalloped potatoes and ham, my friends helped me make mints for the occasion, and we celebrated in style. Paula was happy, which made me happy.

It was hard to believe that we were on the verge of being empty-nesters. Kelly was in his second year of college and working on his pilot's license.

Paula graduated and took a job managing the Groton swimming pool and had plans to attend college in Aberdeen. Michelle was still in high school and worked as a lifeguard for the Groton swimming pool that summer. Everyone was busy as life must go on.

## SNAP FREEZE AND HAIL STORM

The next year passed in a blur. Michelle was busy in her last year of high school, both the other kids were busy in college, Jim was working nonstop, and I was home. And finally, I felt really good.

I spent much of my time helping Jim the best I could, keeping our house, and following Michelle. I also spent much time caring for my mother, who had started to have seizures. She also became increasingly demanding, and with the seizures had also caused her to lose her driver's license.

I felt stuck. Mom felt as if she had paid for everything while I was ill, and so I should obey her demands. She demanded, and I was to oblige. It was a very difficult time with her.

Before I knew it, the spring of 1990 came and brought with it another busy season. Michelle graduated and I planned the party. Jim worked on the farm, and all three kids worked summer jobs.

I felt sorry for myself that summer. I was in the hospital. Then, when I was finally healed and ready to mother, they were working or at college. I tried to shush myself and was determined to enjoy my family.

Although Mom was still not easy to deal with, I began to understand my mother a little better after that. She felt cheated after my father died like I was feeling cheated in the early stages of my empty nest.

As it does, time passed. Michelle attended college in Vermillion, SD and majored in Medical Technology. Paula transferred and earned a degree in Pharmacy. Kelly finished his education with degrees in Business, Economics, and Human Resources. We were so proud of all of them.

Jim continued to be the invisible man, working to keep the farm running, and I did my best to keep busy. I finally felt strong enough and had energy to spare, so I kept myself busy painting farm buildings, keeping house, and spending time with our mothers.

In 1993, we remodeled and moved into the big house. It was quite ironic that when we finally moved into the big house, all our kids were grown and gone.

And then, I noticed my back acting up a bit. I wasn't terribly worried about the twinges of pain, but knew I should make an appointment.

## CORTISONE SHOT

When my appointment day arrived, I sat in the doctor's office waiting to hear what was causing my back pain. We discussed how I felt, and the doctor felt that I should have a cortisone shot. I disagreed. I felt it necessary to figure out what was wrong, not cover up the pain. It was at that appointment where I felt the old cancer fear return. I thought I had overcome, but the fear returned like it had never left.

I should've gotten a second opinion. But I didn't. The doctor was arrogant and obstinate in his treatment plan. He continued to insist that I needed a cortisone shot. I should have listened to my inner spirit. But I gave in.

The cortisone shot was to be given on an outpatient basis the following day. I asked again if he was certain that the pain wasn't caused by cancer. He assured me it wasn't and that the shots wouldn't cause me any worry.

I was put to sleep and the shot was administered, and I was taken to recovery.

I began to notice that my right leg was tingly, like it was asleep. The nurse wasn't worried, so I ate toast and drank juice and was on my way.

Jim and I left and planned to stop for lunch on our way out of town. The tingling in my leg continued to get worse, so I called the doctor's office before we left town. I was told not to worry. The doctor was fairly certain the cortisone shot wouldn't cause the tingling in my leg.

I returned to the doctor a few days later and questioned him again because there was no improvement in my leg. He was adamant that it wasn't the shot.

I couldn't leave. I just sat there in the office and cried. Another doctor who recognized me saw me and suggested that I have a CAT scan to see what the problem was. The rods in my back prevented the CAT scan, but he did schedule me for an MRI the next day. When the results came back, they felt that the scan showed tumors in my lower spine.

I was scheduled for a followup appointment to determine a plan, and was so frustrated with the treatment I'd received. After a heated argument with the surgeon, I insisted that he find out what the scan showed. I was prepped and underwent yet another surgery. Thankfully, the suspected tumors were actually scar tissue. No cancer, thankfully, but I wasn't able to walk.

I entered the hospital with my leg dragging and left in a wheel chair. I started a downward spiral and became very depressed. It was after Christmas, and the kids all had left to return to college, Jim spent most of his time doing chores, and I had lost my ability to drive.

I fought the wheelchair. I was angry at having to use it, and felt that no one understood how hard it was for me. Friends would tell me that they were going bowling or headed off to the mall to shop. I wanted to do all those things, but I couldn't.

Madonna called and I told her how much I hated the wheelchair and how I wanted to walk in the snow and pick up the mail. I told her that people didn't understand what it was like living and working from a wheelchair. I told her that if she were stuck in a wheelchair, then maybe she'd understand.

My big sister, the same woman who shared my bed as a child and prayed me through my chemotherapy took me straight to task. She told me in short order that I should stop feeling sorry for myself and quit wishing her friends the same, unfortunate fate that I had suffered. And with that she hung up on me.

I knew she was right, but I didn't want to accept it. I cried and cried after the phone call. It took some time, but I turned to what had always gotten me through my toughest times. I prayed. I remember sitting in my living room looking out into the spring sun and telling the Lord that I needed his help. I told him that I didn't think I could handle my life anymore and needed guidance to figure out how to live my life in the body that was failing. And it seemed like overnight that my attitude changed. I found the positivity that had pushed me through treatment after treatment. I did my best at living life with my new accommodations. I couldn't always do things as well or as fast as before, but I did my best.

Jim installed hand controls in the car, and allowed me to be mobile again. I no longer would be house bound. That spring brought college graduations for both girls, party planning to celebrate, and a wedding for Michelle, my baby.

The summer was so busy and I enjoyed having the kids near. Kelly was working in Watertown, Paula moved to Brainerd, Minnesota to start her career in pharmacy, Michelle was preparing for marriage and a move across the country, and Jim was still up to his ears in work.

The wedding was beautiful and Michelle made us so very proud that day, and just two days after the wedding, Michelle and her new husband, Shawn left for Portland, Oregon where Shawn was enrolled in classes for Optometry and Michelle accepted a position as a Medical Technologist.

Jim and I were able to hire some help in 1994 and that allowed us the opportunity for a vacation, something we hadn't been able to do for years! We decided to take the train to visit Shawn and Michelle in Portland since school and work made a visit home impossible.

The train ride proved to be a miserable experience, and Jim vowed to never travel by train again, but our time with Shawn and Michelle was so much fun. They seemed incredibly happy and we all took time to see the sights of Portland together.

## HARVEST AND FAMILY

By 1997, we were full time empty-nesters. Our children had grown up and ventured into lives of their own. Jim made a huge change on the farm and sold the cattle, leaving his mornings and evenings free of milking chores. What a change that was for both of us! I was still wheelchair-bound, but I felt good and was able to keep myself busy by helping around the house.

Jim bought me a riding lawn mower with hand controls, and I spent much time outside, my favorite place, mowing the grass and enjoying the summer sun. I had been warned to always carry my cell phone in case I needed help.

During harvest, Jim asked me if I would help speed up the process by driving the combine. My help would save him numerous trips in and out of the combine, and while he was driving the fruits of the harvest back and forth to the grain elevator, I could continue to combine.

We had a few issues in our new system. Because I required his assistance getting into and out of the combine, when he left my lunch on the truck, I was unable to get it. Once, when he was helping me into the tractor, I slipped and and landed on Jim's head. Jim fell to the ground and rolled around in pain while I hung by my hands onto the railing of the combine. I knew he was in pain, but I couldn't help but hang and laugh at our shenanigans.

The kids were all grown up and living their lives, and although they were no longer in my care, I continued to worry about their well being. Kelly and his wife, Erin moved to Texas in hopes of furthering their chosen careers. Paula moved back to Aberdeen and was going through a divorce. Shawn finished school in Portland, became a doctor, and he and Michelle moved to Texas also. Soon after, Michelle announced that they would also be starting a family. I would be a grandmother.

Her joyous announcement took me back to cancer. When I first received the diagnosis, no one expected me to live. At that time, I prayed fervently to just allow me to see my children again. I hoped, but never got my hopes up during that time, that I would be present for their major milestones. And

I made it. I saw all three of my children graduate from high school and college, I attended all of their weddings, and now, I would see grandchildren.

I was over the moon excited to experience my first grandchild. At long last, I would be able to give that baby the quilt that the church group had made for me so long ago when I was in the hospital going through the bone marrow transplant.

Michelle and Shawn had a baby girl, and she was beautiful! They also had a little boy a few years later, and he was a treat as well!

After grandchildren, Jim and I made every excuse to travel to visit Kelly and Michelle, especially during the winter months. The Texas winters were much kinder to our bones. The bonus was that we got to enjoy our grandchildren. Kelly continued to live in Texas as well, so we were able to spend time with him too.

Paula remained in Aberdeen, close to mom and dad, and she blessed us with another granddaughter, a marvel, and we have enjoyed watching her grow and being a presence in her life.

## VEHICLE ACCIDENT

While driving home from one of our Texas visits, Jim and I were traveling through Wichita, Kansas, when an elderly gentleman who was more interested in the much younger woman sitting next to him than driving his car, ran a red light and smashed into our vehicle.

I didn't think I was hurt, but the crash was the final straw, leaving me completely paralyzed from the waist down. The black wheel chair that I'd used since the botched cortisone shot several years previous was no longer suitable to my needs. Before the accident, I was able to use my good leg to move about in the chair because arthritis in my hands made it impossible to push myself about. After the car accident, I no longer had the use of my good leg.

While waiting for a new wheelchair, I tried to stay positive. I relied solely on Jim to move from place to place. I was determined to gain some independence once again, and I decided that I wanted a bright colored, electric chair that turned easily.

We spoke to a man selling wheelchairs and he assured me that he could appropriately fit the chair and promised me that my new, cherry-colored wheels would be delivered within weeks. Additionally, we ordered a van that was fit with hand controls that allowed me to drive and a lift that could move my chair into and out of the van. It even locked in place allowing me to drive right from my chair.

All of the accommodations were so appreciated, but the cost was much more than the settlement from the car accident that caused my predicament. The chair offered me some freedom. I was finally able to move about the house and do housework, and life became somewhat normal. But the pain in my back continued to worsen.

Unfortunately, the wheelchair salesman who promised that he properly fit me to my new cherry-red wheels had not done a good job, and since I was paralyzed, all feeling had left the lower half of my body. Because of the poor fit, my body slipped from side-to-side and front-to-back causing bed

sores that cut clear to the bone.
I went back to the faithful doctors in my hometown for treatment. After eight months with little relief, the pain and depression were making me miserable. I spent the majority of that year in bed praying for recovery

We fought with the owner of the wheelchair company and were eventually given a refund for the ill-fitting chair, but only after threatening to meet with an attorney. The money, most definitely, didn't change the fact that I was bedridden.

My daughter, Michelle, who worked in a hospital in Texas convinced us that we should allow the doctors at her hospital to treat the bed sores. The doctors looked at my bedsores and took me off to surgery where they scraped the bone and added tissue to the skin so that the sore would grow together.

The local doctors left the bed sores open, allowing E. coli to enter my bloodstream. The Texas doctors checked me over from end to end. They identified all the places that I'd had cancer, and showed me a spot in my brain that had once been cancerous lesions, something I didn't know.

There were so many times throughout my life that I felt the presence of God and knew that He took care of me, but that knowledge brought me back to the lady who came into my home and prayed with me so many years ago. I remembered the warmth that flowed through my body, the bright light, and the figure of the man and the proof that God granted me a miracle came rushing back.

I spent the next five weeks healing in the Texas hospital. The pain in my legs was causing me much agony and the doctors were unable to do anything to relieve it. The car accident had caused tremendous nerve damage and brought with it pain.

The hospital brought in someone to correctly fit me for a wheelchair that would not result in bedsores. The new model had hand controls and a lift so that I could reach the top of my stove and still do dishes. Lucky me! The wheelchair was big and bulky and made mobility difficult.

I struggled to roll over in bed and move from my chair to the couch. I wasn't strong enough to move myself using the hand bars, so I relied on Jim for everything.

I struggled greatly during that time. I was angry about the accident and the botched cortisone shot that had put me in the wheel chair. I was so very sad that, once again, I had to redefine my life. And on top of it all, the paralysis made controlling my bowels difficult too.

An appointment was made with a specialist who suggested that I undergo surgery to put in a colostomy. After the surgery, the colostomy was nothing but trouble. The nurse removed the staples too early causing bleeding and a trip to the ER, I contracted an infection that turned out to be MRSA-VRE, and required months of antibiotics, and the colostomy didn't seem to work. The bag wouldn't stay on and I was getting BM all over all the time. It was extremely difficult to get an appointment with the specialist who had done the surgery, and when I finally did, he told me that the surgery would need to be repeated and corrected.

Although I was ready to get the surgery over with, my husband and daughter decided to take me to Texas so that the colostomy could be properly fixed. I spent some time working with Home Health to help shrink the colon hole and help me change the bags. The surgery was finally performed and the colostomy was corrected. A surgery that should have taken one week, took over five months.

Michelle, Shawn and Kelly had bought tickets for the grandchildren to be in South Dakota that Christmas, but because of the surgery, we would be stuck in Texas. Kelly graciously stayed with us since we couldn't go home, but Shawn, Michelle and the kids made the trip and were able to visit his parents. Even Paula planned to come to Texas to spend the holiday with us. We were so happy to be together, even if it wasn't Christmas exactly.

The past decade has brought me so many joys and some sorrow. I learned to live with the wheelchair and colostomy accommodations, and although I would have chosen a different fate if I'd had the choice, I have accepted it.

## Barb's Journey by Barbara Pray

On the occasion that I feel myself getting down, I pray. On the occasions, and there have been many, that bring me great joy, I pray. If my life has taught me anything, it has taught me that my life, my fate, and my eternal happiness are all due to my faith in the Lord.

Although my life has been difficult, overwhelming, and at times I wished for my own death, I wouldn't have chosen a different path. I survived a death sentence, not without scars, but I got to live my life. When I was diagnosed, I prayed for life. I prayed that I would be able to be the mother I so desperately wanted to be, and my prayers were answered.

I lived my life and on May 5, 2014, I celebrated my 30 year anniversary as a cancer survivor. By this time, you have read my story and know the struggle I faced. I am proud of that fight! And I am thankful, thankful for the gift of time, a wonderful, loyal and loving husband who has never let me down, beautiful children and grandchildren, and friends and family.

Life has never been easy, but I am still so happy that I got to live it.

# 2014
# Epilogue

Even now, staying healthy is difficult. In the best years, I have several bouts of pneumonia and often spend time in the hospital. With the toll that has been taken on my body over the years, I suppose that is to be expected. Recently, I was feeling ill and made an appointment with the doctor. What I thought would be routine turned into a hospital stay that put a great scare into my whole family.

The doctor hospitalized me, and it was probably a good thing. I quickly became septic and my oxygen levels dropped dangerously low. I had to be intubated just to keep me breathing. The doctors thought that my situation was so dire that all my children were called in to spend what could've been my last days here on earth. But, as with all of the miracles in my life, the grace of God pulled me through, and I am still here.

## LETTERS FROM MY CHILDREN AND GRANDDAUGHTER (UNEDITED)

My name is Kelly the oldest of three children. On May 8th, 1984 I was 15 in the 9th grade.

Prior to my Mom's diagnosis of cancer on May 8th, 1984 our family was somewhat close. Specifically my relationship with my Mom was much closer than my relationship with my Dad. If I needed something or had a question I would turn to my Mother. Never or very seldom did I ask my Dad anything unless it was related to the chores or work that I would assist with on the farm. We ate dinner every night at 7:30 as a family after my Dad and I finished with chores of feeding and milking the cows. We were a very routine family eating meat, potato, and gravy. Although we ate together, I really don't remember any deep conversation. After dinner my sisters would clean-up and we would all descend into the basement family room to watch that evening programming and share a bowl of popcorn. We would pretty much do this 7 days a week. It sounds maybe a little boring or mundane, but it was what we did as a family. Everyone worked hard and this was time for us to relax as a family.

One year prior to May 8th and leading up to that day, we did see a dynamic change in our family. My Mom had a lot of back pain and it lead to more tension in our family. She spent more and more time lying down, crying, and yelling. I remember using the restroom in the middle of night and my mom would be sleeping standing in the corner of the room near the bathroom. She would tell me her back hurt too bad to lay down on it. Sometimes she would ask me to rub her back while she had tears in her eyes. So I would rub her back for a few minutes, but as a 15 year old that was not really what you wanted to spend your time doing. After a few minutes, of course I would begin to complain and she would say that's ok. Of course today I regret not spending more time rubbing her back.

She was going to the doctors more and would return crying. She never complained to us kids, but spent less time talking to us about school, and friends. But when morning arrived she was always at work. We learned a lot of things from our parents, but one thing is for sure is that you need to work hard. My Dad told me two things about work: 1. "If you cannot see what needs to be done and do it then you are not a great worker" 2. "If you have to tell everyone how much work you are doing then you are not doing much." My mom worked at the school as a baker and would start work early maybe 5:00 am and worked until approximately 2:00 pm. I remember she would be in so much pain after work that she could not drive the 8 miles home. Instead she would go to my grandmother's apartment 2 blocks away and lay down. I don't remember why I was at my grandmother's apartment in the early afternoon maybe it was a half day of school. My mom was lying on the coach and she was crying, "I can't do this anymore and I need these doctors to find out what is wrong with me. It is not in my head. Why, why do they tell me it is in my head?" I walked over to the coach and she grabbed my hand with both of her hands and squeezed hard.

Saturday May 5$^{th}$, 1984 my Mom went into the hospital in the early evening. This was the last time she would be home for a long time. I remember visiting her in the hospital on Sunday, which was actually a little fun for us kids at the time. I think mainly because we always got to eat out, which was a nice treat (usually Burger King). We kids also did not understand the severity of the issue, and we were never really told how sick she really was.

I had a science project due Wednesday, so when I got home from the hospital on Sunday late afternoon I had to work on that prior to my chores. The project was to drop an egg from a two story building and keep it from breaking. If your egg did not break or crack then the winner was determined by the overall size of the package. I was pretty happy with my design as it was very small and compact. I guess I was getting about a 50% success rate on the drop, so I was hopeful that I had a chance.

## Barb's Journey by Barbara Pray

Tuesday night May 8th our grandparents were asked to bring us kids up to the hospital. I was testing my science project by throwing my egg into the air. I brought my egg drop design with me to show my Mom. I knew she would like it and maybe even recommend some changes. I was not prepared for what we were about to receive that night. Arriving at the hospital it was a little crazy. I don't remember exactly how it came out or who even told me. I just remember that she had a tumor in the 4th stage. I was thinking to myself you mean cancer, but did not know what 4th stage meant. There was a lot of crying, but I never for one moment thought that my Mom could die. I don't remember crying, but had tears in my eyes as it was hard to watch my Mom cry. Then they told us that they needed to fly her to Minneapolis the next day.

The next morning my sisters and I went to school. I was still in shock and a little bit of a daze. Not until science class, which was a morning class, did I realize I left my egg design in my grandparent's car. The rule was you forget your project and you have to do extra work for the day on vertical acceleration and you got a "C" on your project if you did the extra work. In class, I was asked for my egg design, I explained that my Mom was diagnosed with a tumor and is flying to Minneapolis today. I had left my design in my Grandparent's car. I was told to go get my book from my locker along with two other people (who forgot there design) as I was required to do the extra work so I can get my "C". I remember walking down the hallway toward my locker. I open the locker door and began to cry. I grabbed my coat and headed to the front office where I explained that I was not feeling well and wanted to go home. I asked them to call my Grandparents because my Mom and Dad were at the hospital. My Grandparents picked me up at the school and took me with them to the hospital where we met my Mom and Dad. Shortly after we arrived they took her to the Aberdeen airport and put her on a small turboprop airplane to fly her to Minneapolis. As tears rolled down my Mom's eyes she told me just before she was going to the plane to be loaded, "I love you, take care of your sisters, and I will be home soon. " My Grandparents and I watch the plane roll to the end of the runway then start down it picking up speed and eventually taking off. My Grandma was crying, which again caused me to have tears in my eyes. We watched the plane role to the left overhead and fly back toward us on its way to Minneapolis.

Side note: The next day, I told my Grandparents I did not want to go to school. They never questioned why. To be honest, I really did not want to go because in science class they were going to be dropping the eggs from the school. This is one of those projects that every year you watched the classes out the windows of the school dropping the eggs. I was very excited about the project, but because I did not turn in my project I had nothing to drop. Plus I did not want to see my teacher. I really don't know what I got for a grade on that project and I never asked. I also never did the extra work, but I did get an apology from my teacher when I returned to school. I am sure as a teacher he has heard 100 different lies and excuses of why someone forgot their project, but unfortunately mine was true. My Mom did have cancer and I left it in my Grandparent's car.

I really don't remember how long my Mom and Dad were gone before we saw them again. We kids moved into my Grandparent's home, and I got into my routine. I would drive my sisters to school in the morning and bring them home at night. I would have something to eat then go outside to feed the cattle. Return to the house and eat with my sisters and grandparents. The differences I remember from being at home is that Grandma would wake us up and ask what we wanted for breakfast. My Mom worked in the morning so we got up on our own (ok my sisters would wake me sometimes) and we made our own breakfast. Although I liked my Grandma making breakfast, I think we learned responsibility by getting up on our own, which was a valuable lesson to learn. But the biggest difference was just not having my Mom and Dad home. My parents would call about once a week and we would talk to them for a few minutes as it was expensive to call long distance, but again my mom told me she would be home soon. So again, I never thought about her dying.

The next 4 years while I was in high school my Mom was in and out of the hospital and it hard to put the time line together for me of when and what was going on with my Mom's health. I remember some key events for me during this time, but I don't remember exactly when it was in my Mom's sickness. She had cancer then it was cleared, but even now the cancer is gone, but she still today battles the effects of cancer. I don't think from 1985 to today has she ever gone a full year without spending a period of time in the hospital. That is over 30 years of not having one year without being in the hospital, and I don't see that changing for her.

My Mom and Dad came home from the Minneapolis hospital on one occasion. Mom was very ill at this time. Again I don't know the timing in her sickness of this day, but she was lying on the coach and she was in a lot of pain. She asked for her bible while she was crying. The bible was lying on the end table. I was in the kitchen which was adjacent to where she was lying on the coach. My Dad handed her the bible. I assumed she was going to use it for prayer as she had done in the past. She had a lot of paper in the bible that did not mean much to me until this day. As she opened the bible she found a piece of paper that had a corner of it torn off. Then she said to my Dad, "Who tore this?" She was crying as she said it. Dad of course did not know who tore it, but I did. Earlier that day a friend of mine called to give me a phone number. I grabbed a pen and paper from the bible and wrote it down. Then I looked at the paper and it was a copy of a music song with notes. This would not mean much to our family as none of us were musical. So I never thought about it. To me it was scrap paper. I heard my Mom say something to my Dad, but I could not understand as she was crying even loader. I could only make out that she could not understand who would tear this paper. Then my Dad started yelling at me, "Who tore this?" I knew this was something important to them. I admitted that I tore it, but I tried to explain that I did not know what it was. That is when my Dad yelled, "Why would you tear up the music that Mom wants played at her funeral?" At that moment is the first time that I ever thought my Mom could die. I tore up the song she wanted played at her funeral. I went to the basement in my room and closed my door and cried for long time thinking my Mom was going to die. Up to this point I never thought once that she would die.

At this time things changed for me. I now took it much more serious and appreciated the time I have with my Mom and Dad. I also realized that our family dynamics had changed as well. This was enforced on one of our trips to Minneapolis. My Dad was home, but my Mom was in the hospital. He was driving us back to Minneapolis to visit my mom. While in the car driving my Dad talked to us kids about how important we are to him. He explained to us that there is nothing more important to Mom and him than us kids. He told us he loved us and would do whatever he could for us kids. I don't remember my Dad ever saying anything like this in the past. He wants us to go to college and if he has to work 3 jobs to pay for it he would do it. I don't know why he did this. Maybe he thought Mom would not be around much longer, and he wanted to open up with us kids. But whatever the reason from this day forward I was never afraid to ask my Dad questions again. I also recognized that everyone's role in the family was changing to the situation.

We made 3 other trips to Minneapolis and the first one; I remember driving to Minneapolis with my sister's and my two grandmas'. It was shortly after we finished school in late May 1985. I split driving time with my Grandma Wenschlag, but when we got into Minneapolis I was driving. This was a big deal for me as I was 15 years old and the only roads I had driven were gravel and the paved roads around our small town. I had only been to Minneapolis one other time and that was with my youth church group so this was a big trip for us. Mom was very sick, but I actually remember her being very good spirits. They would not allow her to leave her room; so much of the time we spent visiting. I remember the hospital being very plain with no decorations or anything that made you feel good. It was very poor looking compared to the Aberdeen Hospital. It surprised me to see it in such poor condition. It is much different if you go to the U of M Hospital today.

We made one trip to Minneapolis with my Aunt who had family in Minneapolis, so that worked for both of us. Another trip we made with my Dad's cousins, who spent time visiting with my parents. My mom was not allowed to get up nor did she have the strength to get up. Most of our trips to Minneapolis, my Mom was in good spirits except the one time we visited her after her back surgery. I don't know if they put rods in her back or took the infected ones out. I want to say they took them out. She had gotten out of surgery and they had forgotten to give her the right pain killer and she was in a lot of pain. I reached down to touch her hand and as I touched she began to say owe, owe, owe… I felt so bad, she is already in a lot of pain and I just made it worse by touching her hand. It was very hard to watch. It took some time, but they finally got her the pain killer she needed then she began to relax and sleep.

While my Mom was sick she told me later that she would make goals for herself. The first one was to make it home for Christmas, then she would achieve that then she would make a new one. One of her goals was to make it to my high school graduations. It was shortly after one of her back surgeries. She had gotten home just one day prior to my graduation and at graduation she rolled into the school in a wheelchair and a back brace. She sat in the center aisle of the gymnasium unable to stand. I have pictures of me in my graduation gown and Mom sitting in her chair. Another goal achieved. Then she would make a new goal and lived to see all of us graduate from high school, and collage making every one of them.

Now that I am older and look back on this time I am more and more amazed. I think about the stress and challenges my parents endured. My parents always say how proud of us kids they are, but I have done very little compared to my Mom and Dad. They are both very strong people. Mom fought cancer and won, but it did not end there. She has to battle her back pain and the challenges of being confined to a wheelchair every day. But if you meet my Mom you will very seldom see her any different than you and me. She is always on the move cleaning her house, having coffee parties, or going to town. She is my inspiration. My Dad is also an amazing man being with my Mom during all of this and making things a little easier for her. My Dad is my aspiration. I love them both.

Kelly

## Barb's Journey by Barbara Pray

I was thirteen years old in the 7th grade about a year and ½ older than my daughter (Alexa) is right now. I was home that evening with my sister and brother getting my things ready for a Jr. High track meet the next day. My dad called and told my brother that my grandparents would be picking us kids up and taking us to the hospital in Aberdeen to see my mom. My mom was going to the Doctors a lot….I wasn't surprised to hear she was in the hospital. I wasn't real excited about going to the hospital that evening because I had a lot of homework and I was getting ready for track and field day.

When we arrived at the hospital my mom's room was dark and there were a lot of family and friend outside her room. I remember thinking this was kind of odd. "What's the occasion?" Dad met us at the door of mom's hospital room I could tell he was scared and upset. Mom was lying in bed eyes filled with tears. I just figured she must be in pain again; however, that wasn't the case. Mom told us that they had found a tumor in her back and that she would have to go to Minneapolis to the University hospital. I didn't understand what a tumor was. I've heard the word tumor but didn't associate it with cancer. It wasn't until the next evening when dad called my grandparents, who we were staying with, to tell us that Mom was having emergency surgery to remove some tumor off her spine because her legs were starting to go numb. I didn't understand why my grandmother and brother were so worried. My thought was just take all if it out so she can come home. That's when by brother explained to me what a tumor and cancer were and how sick mom was. I still didn't understand it completely…Mom will be OK she's going to get better and be home soon.

To my surprise that wasn't the case. Over the next six months mom just keep getting worse. She was weak, in pain, lost a lot of weight, lost her hair, and always feeling nauseous. Between traveling to Minneapolis for treatments she would lay on the sofa in the living room and tell my sister how to make gravy for dinner. My sister and I made a deal that if she cooked…I would clean up. I remember fighting with my siblings when we were smaller but not around my mom when she was home, maybe because we knew she wasn't well.

Mom and Dad didn't let us kids know how serious mom's cancer was. I never felt my mom was anywhere close to death until December of 1984. Everybody came to our house for Christmas that year. I thought this was great; however, there was something going on! Whenever anyone left to go home mom would get very emotional and so would the others? Why? That was when I demanded to know what was going on. My dad explained to me how serious mom's condition was and that after the first of the year she would be returning to Minneapolis to go through a bone marrow transplant. He explained that there's a chance that she might not live through it……I broke down into tears. For the first time the thought that mom might not live crossed my mind! I prayed to God to not take our mom from us. I remember being angry with God for allowing my mom to get cancer. Mom always went to church and prayed. She was kind and generous to everyone. Why would God want to take her from us?

I remember traveling to Minneapolis about once every 3-4 weeks to see mom and dad. One time my Grandparents took us. Another time my Dad's cousin and his wife took us. Each time we went I wished we were going for a vacation instead of to the hospital. It was so boring, Mom was in isolation so she couldn't leave her room and we had to wear masks and gowns when we went to see her. Whenever we would go in her room I remember looking at the piece of paper that hung on the cork board. This is where they recorded her White Blood Cell (WBC) , Red Blood Cell (RBC), and Platelet count. I didn't know what these numbers meant, but I remember we had a goal to reach before mom could come home with us.

While in the hospital mom made me a purple puppy out of yarn, had I known how much work this project was for mom I would have taken better care of it so I still had it today. As a child I took so much of what my parents did for me for granted. I see this now with my own child and wish I would have been different.

I remember mom and dad talking and sometimes fighting about money and the lack thereof. I wanted to help, but didn't know how. I remember my older brother telling my sister and me not to ask mom and dad for money if we really needed money for something we should come to him. We didn't need much we stayed with my grandparents and rode the bus home from school every night. We didn't partake in any extra activies while mom was going through treatment. I quit playing piano, which I wasn't very good at anyway. I tried to do well in school because this was important to my mom. She always said, "Do your best in school, it's one of the most important journeys you will take in your life……. It will decide your future".

When we received the news that mom's bone marrow was free of cancer we were beyond excited. Over the next 5 years mom returned to the University Hospital several times for tests to make sure the cancer didn't resurface. Every time she left I would fastback to the 2 years of hell she went through and pray that God would keep her free of this awful disease.

After mom got her strength back life seemed to be back to normal. I played a little high school basketball, on the cheer squad, and enjoyed going to high school. After high school I decided to go to Northern State University and become an elementary education teacher. Before registering for classes in the fall I decided to change my major to Pharmacy. I found Chemistry and the study of medicine interesting. Even though I knew it was God that put my mom's cancer in remission I was still curious about all the science of medicine.

I went to Northern State University for 1 year than transferred to South Dakota State University and applied to Pharmacy School. I was accepted and started my journey to become a pharmacist. My last year of pharmacy school involved clinical rotations two of the three rotations I did in Aberdeen; therefore, I lived at home with mom and dad. This is when I realized mom wasn't doing well. She seemed to be in a lot of pain and she couldn't walk without dragging one leg. Being older now I understood more of what was going on. The damage done to my mother's body by the chemotherapy and radiation was taking its toll. No matter how much pain mom was in or how crappy she felt she would do anything for her children.

Mom always worried about how she looked when she had to walk with canes or use a wheelchair. She would always say she looked like an old lady. I never saw that! She is beautiful. I struggled with myself image throughout high school and college especially being overweight. I think back how selfish that was of me. I'm worried about an extra 20 lbs. when I can fix that, but mom can't fix her legs or get rid of the pain. Even today when I start to get down on myself… I remind myself of those who are worse off than me.

Mom is a sick lady. She's in and out of the hospital often because of infections and pain. There have been a couple of occasions since she's been in remission that I thought God was going to take my mom. I keep pleading to God that I'm not ready to let her go. She plays such an important role in mine and my daughter's life. Sometimes I feel selfish in wanting to hang on to her because in heaven I know she'll be able to walk, run, and dance. When these close calls come around I just pray that the Lord will give me another day, month, or years with this incredible lady I call MOM. He's answered my prayers and for that I thank him.

I thank God for giving me the strongest mother in the world & the most caring and giving father to stand beside mom through this journey.

I am now married to a wonderful man who reminds me of my father in so many ways. I have a beautiful girl who I adore and I am trying to teach her all the valuable lessons my parents have taught me. I work as a pharmacist and love learning the advances in medicine but will never lose sight of the real cure…GOD! Paula

I'm Michelle, the youngest of three. I was 12 years old and just finishing 6th grade year when I found out my mom had cancer. My Mom was always fun, she was the mom that every girl wanted her friends to meet. She was young and pretty which seemed important to me at the time. But during my sixth grade year my Mom wasn't the same. She was tired a lot and didn't feel well. She had a harder time keeping up with everything around the home. My sister and I always worked around the house. Every Saturday morning we would clean the house from top to bottom. It was expected of us and we always did it, may have complained, but we always did it. Mom was the one that made sure we had everything we needed; groceries in the home, dinner on the table, clean clothes to wear to school and took care of us when we were sick. In April of 1984 I got the stomach flu and was home from school for a few days. Mom worked at the school and Dad worked on the farm. Mom always took care of me when I was sick but this time was different, Mom was to sick herself. She would come home from work and didn't feel well so I was left to take care of myself. I became very dehydrated and couldn't stop vomiting so Mom had to take me to the doctor. It was a Saturday and our family doctor wasn't there so I saw a new doctor that day, he was fresh out of medical school. Ironically, this is the same doctor that finally listened to Mom and diagnosed her cancer one month later and is still her family doctor today. I do remember thinking the hospital was great because they waited on me hand and foot. Mom would come up to the hospital after work to check on me. She was in a lot of pain at this time, I remember getting out of my hospital bed so she could lie down because her back hurt so bad. This was when I realized mom wasn't herself anymore, she smiled less and cried more.

In May, Mom went into the hospital. I really don't remember this except going up one night to visit. My sister, brother and I were walking done the long hallway to Mom's hospital room. Her room was at the end of the hall. Many of our family and friend were sitting in the hallway outside Mom's room and everyone was quiet and looked very sad. I remember hearing the words that Mom was sick and had a tumor in her back but I had no idea what it really meant. They told us that mom would be going to Minneapolis to the hospital but that didn't seem to bother me because I was just in the hospital and it was great. I was starting my adolescent years and illness and death weren't something that I thought about. I was more focused on my friends at school then anything and that is what my parents wanted for me, to continue on without feeling any different.

It was Mother's Day and Mom and Dad had been gone for a few day, they promised to call us kids at Grandma and Grandpa's house so we could wish Mom a Happy Mother's Day. When Dad called I was hoping to wish Mom a Happy Mother's day but it was to tell my grandparents that Mom was going in for emergency surgery to remove the tumor off her back. I didn't really understand the seriousness of it but I remember my Grandma acting very worried. We didn't get to wish Mom a Happy Mother's Day so I made her a card and mailed it to her.

I remember when Mom and Dad were away I would make cards and send them. I thought of them all the time but never realizing how sick Mom really was. I made her funny cards because Mom always liked to laugh. One time, I made her a pair of glasses that look like a pig. It had pig ears and pig nose attached to the glasses. Not sure why I chose to make her those but Mom always like homemade things from her children and I just wanted to make her smile.

When we lived with Grandma and Grandpa I spent a lot of time with my brother. He was 3 and half years older then me and I was always just his little sister. But when Mom and Dad were away Kelly stepped in to take care of my sister and I. I became very close to him. We would sit upstairs in his room at the farm house and talk and listen to music. He would talk to me about girls he liked and I would listen. It was pretty cool because he was in high school and I was going into junior high.

In junior high my friends would complain about there Mom"s getting onto them for this and that and I remember thinking to myself, "I wish my mom was home to get onto me." I learned at a young age to not take things for granted. This is one of the many things I learned from Mom's fight with cancer.

Mom came home sometime in the summer of 1984 and my chores around the house increase. My sister started to do laundry and I learned how to cook. Mom was to weak to help me in the kitchen because this was during her chemo treatments. She would teach me from the couch were she spent most of her time. If I wanted her to see how something looked I would carry the pan to her and ask, "Does it need more milk or does it look okay". I guess it's not the most traditional way to learn how to cook but it was how I learned. Dad worked all the time when he wasn't with Mom at the hospital. He was a very serious man and worked very hard his whole life. It was during Mom's illness that I saw the softer side of my father. He was very quiet but after Mom became sick he showed a lot more emotion and affection to us kids. The year before Mom got sick we went on a family vacation to California. It was awesome. On that trip I got to know Dad, I called him the "Vacation Dad". He went swimming with us, played games, and took up to Disneyland. I just remember after Mom got sick Dad became :Vacation Dad" all the time. He continued to work hard but I knew he was there for me if I ever needed anything.

Christmas 1984 Mom found out that she would need a bone marrow transplant. I was completely unaware of what that meant. I thought it was a continuation of her chemo that was going to take the cancer away. Never though Mom's fight with cancer did I ever know that Mom could die. I know my parents kept this from me because I was only 12. I thought that was a great Christmas because everyone was at our house. All my grandparents, cousins, and aunts and uncles. I loved being around my family and I thought it was great to have everyone there for Christmas. I didn't know everyone was there because they thought it was Mom's last one. I feel guilty for that today but I know my parents kept things from me so that I wouldn't worry.

When Mom had her bone marrow transplant it was in the winter of 1985. We went to visit Mom and Dad at the University Hospital in Minneapolis. It was exciting because we hadn't seen them since Christmas. It was in February and it was my 13th birthday. Mom always made our birthdays special. She would make us chicken noodle soup, our favorite, and our grandparents would come for dinner. We always had cake, ice cream, and a present but this birthday was different, Mom was in the hospital recovering from her bone marrow transplant, but I knew Mom would try to make it special. She asked me what I wanted for my birthday and I knew that money was tight, but I loved basketball and I really wanted one. We were walking up the sidewalk to the hospital and I was looking up at the hospital room windows. I saw a window that had decorations it in and I said, "That's mom's room... I know it". When I arrived into her room it was all decorated with streamers and balloons for my birthday and on her bed was a present wrapped in brown paper bag wrapping. I was excited and I hope I showed Mom and Dad how excited I was. At the time, I had know idea how difficult it was for Mom to decorate that room but later she told me how much energy that took. I got my basketball and it was a very special birthday but what made it special was that I got to celebrate with my Mom and Dad. They were gone for 3 months while Mom was getting her blood counts back up. I remember Mom talking about where her blood counts needed to be before she could come home and watching her receive blood products while we visited. I thought it was so interesting that they could give her blood products like that, I wondered why they couldn't just give her enough blood products so her counts would get up and she could just come home. I didn't understand all this medical stuff yet. Mom and Dad finally came home, but Mom was very weak. She continued to fight and spent a lot of time praying. We all did, prayer became a routine for me. Whenever it was quiet I would ask God to heal my mom. I know the doctors were put in place by Him to heal her and it was through prayer that all the stars alined to allow Mom to stay with us.

After her fight with cancer her struggles continued. She went through many back surgeries throughout my high school career. She continued to fight through and recovered from each one. I went off to college in 1990 at the University of South Dakota to pursue my degree in Medical Technology. My parents always told me how important it was to get an education. Mom would tell me that no one can take your education from you. My third year of college I received a phone call from home. She was suffering a lot with back pain again and was going to the doctors to find out why. By this time she had many major reconstructive back surgery to repair

the damage caused by the cancer so back pain was part of her daily routine but the pain was getting worse. She was seeking help from her family doctor and they were concern that her cancer was back. She told me on the phone that day and I sat on my floor and cried. I understood the word "Cancer" this time. It ended up being adhesion's from all her surgeries and once again the Lord answered our prayers.
In 1994 I got married to Shawn Kelly, my college sweetheart, and we moved to Portland Oregon following our wedding. That was a hard day to leave my family. We had been through a lot together and we were very close. Mom was starting to see side effects from the radiation damage and she was starting to loose feeling in her legs. At my wedding she walk with a cane, which she hated, but it kept her from falling and her one leg was starting to drag. My husband and I returned home for a visit the summer of 1995 and Dad warned me that Mom's legs had gotten worse. I had not seen her for about a year but I thought that it couldn't be that much different. I departed the plane and saw Mom at the end of the tarmac and she was standing there being held up by her arm canes. It was then that I realized Dad was telling me the truth. Mom could no longer walk without arm canes. I watched her struggle to move and saw that it took a lot of effort with her canes. It was upsetting to see how she had degraded since I left one year ago. She had completely lost her feeling in her one leg. She used her wheelchair 80% of the time. I remember initially being very upset but then when I saw all the things she continued to do it made me realize that this is just part of her day. She was still happy, laughing, and working around the home as if there was nothing wrong. I am sure she made it look okay so we wouldn't worry. She was very good at that.

In 2001, Mom lost both legs and struggle with becoming a paraplegic. As an adult and watching the struggles my parent go through each day has been eye opening. I have watched her struggle with her health for 30 years. She is an amazing women that has concurred many struggles. She was lucky because she had a loving husband that has been by her side since the beginning. Dad has always been a quiet man and you know the old adage "Actions speaks louder than words."? Dad lived that adage. He has supported Mom and taken care of her for 30 years. It's a nontraditional love story that I am very proud of.

I now live in Plano Texas, a suburb of Dallas, with my husband, Shawn, and two children, Maddie 13 and Chris 11. I realize that my daughter is the same age I was when Mom was fighting cancer and I understand why my parents didn't want me to know the magnitude of her disease. I have chosen a career path in healthcare because of my mothers fight. I now teach health science at a local high school in the Dallas area. Mom is a cancer survivor and I thank God each day for that. She has seen me graduate from high school, college, marriage, children, and soon her grandchildren will be graduating from high school. She has seen it all and I have had the pleasure of getting to know my mother as an adult. There has been many times I have called Mom for advice and realize how lucky I am that she is still here to answer. When I think back on growing up, I will always remember Mom being sick but I never let it change how I saw her. Even when she was at her weakest or today when she struggles to live from her wheelchair, I will always see her as the fun, pretty mom that I want to introduce to my friends. Thank you Mom and Dad for all that you have done for me. I love you both very much.

Michelle

## Barb's Journey by Barbara Pray

My favorite memories of my grandma are… Going to Storybook Land in Aberdeen with her and my cousins Maddie and Chris. I remember I was always scared of the lion's den, so I would always want her to go first. Then there was the witch's castle. I would always wonder how the "real witch" got up to the top of the castle. My cousins and I would look for the "hidden stairs" and would play out the Wizard of Oz.

I also loved when she would take me to the Groton Park and the Groton Pool. One day when we went to the park I thought it would be fun to swing in a baby swing. Unfortunately I was about 3 years to big, so the outcome was me getting stuck. When I wanted to get out I couldn't because I was pretty well stuck in there. So my grandma tried to get me out but it was hard for her to do in a wheel chair. So a nice man at the park helped me get out.

Grandma was more than just another women with cancer, she was a mother and a wife. She had to fight for her family. My mom was about my age when Grandma I found out she had cancer.

Grandma is my role model we almost lost her not to long ago and if she wasn't here now I don't know what I would do. She buys me some of the nicest things I own. I really appreciate the money and gifts, but that's not what I love the most…. it is the love that comes with them I love. I will get random calls from her and I love talking to her.

What I have learned from my grandma's sickness is: Don't let fear and cancer keep you from living life you need to fight it. Grandma is an example that cancer doesn't always win you can fight and beat it

Alexa Rossman Age: 11

Barb (I call her, Mimi) is my grandmother. I got a call from Mimi a while ago asking me to write something about myself so I'll give it a try. Hi, my name is Maddie I am 13 (14 in 8 days). Anyway I live with my younger brother, Mom, Dad, 2 dogs, and one cat. So know you know who I am let's get into my story.

I guess you could say I live a basic life. Go to school, see friends, study, play sports, and most of all spend time on my phone all day long! But things changed about a year ago when I started to take insulin injections, testing for ketones, and testing my glucose. If you don't know what it is I'm talking about to sum it up in about 5 words I'm a type one diabetic. Know don't think it's the same as type 2! There is a big difference. My body's immune system attacked my beta cells in my pancreas which caused my body to stop creating insulin which helps break down sugars within my body. Type 2 is when you blood cells don't recognize the insulin your body is creating which is curable...my type however is not.

It was an early morning and I had a doctor's appointment because I had all these  unusual symptoms , polyuria (peeing A LOT), polyphagia (eating A LOT and still being hungry), and polydipsia (drinking A LOT of water). When I got to the doctor's office with my dad I did a urine test then the doctor came in he said my urine was full of glucose but they were still waiting for my blood results to come in to be sure. A few minutes later the blood test came back and my glucose was sky high which confirmed my diagnosis, Type 1 diabetic. When the doctors told me it hit hard, I didn't know what they were talking about all I knew was I was different from everyone else...or so I thought. After my 3 days staying at the local hospital I took classes to learn how to control my diabetes. There I met a lot of boys and girls my age with the same disease and at school I found out a few people had it too, I wasn't alone anymore. All these people I met taught me new things, but one girl in my grade led me to the best place ever, Camp Sweeney. A place where people of all ages from 5-18 go to learn about their diabetes. This was the only place I have ever felt normal. Everyone is testing their glucose, taking insulin injections, and testing for ketones! Camp, even though I have only gone for 2 sessions, has taught me so many things that I never knew. Camp is my home away from home, the place where everyone understands me.

Mimi has been in a wheelchair my whole life but I never really looked at Mimi being different ... she is just my grandma that happens to be in a wheelchair. I guess it is kinda like me, I am no different than my friends... I just happen to have a pancreas that doesn't make insulin. I wish Mimi had her own Camp Sweeney, where she could feel normal.

Madeline

What I like about my Mimi is when she comes to my hockey games. When she is there I always see her in the stands with a smile on her face. I love when we go to Storybook Land. I was scared of the lions cave. I like when we go to the Aberdeen Wings game.

Christopher Kelly Age: 11

Grandpa Jim, Grandma Mimi and Alexa

Alexa Rossman, age 11.

Left:: Barb before back surgery.
Right: Mrs. Hope

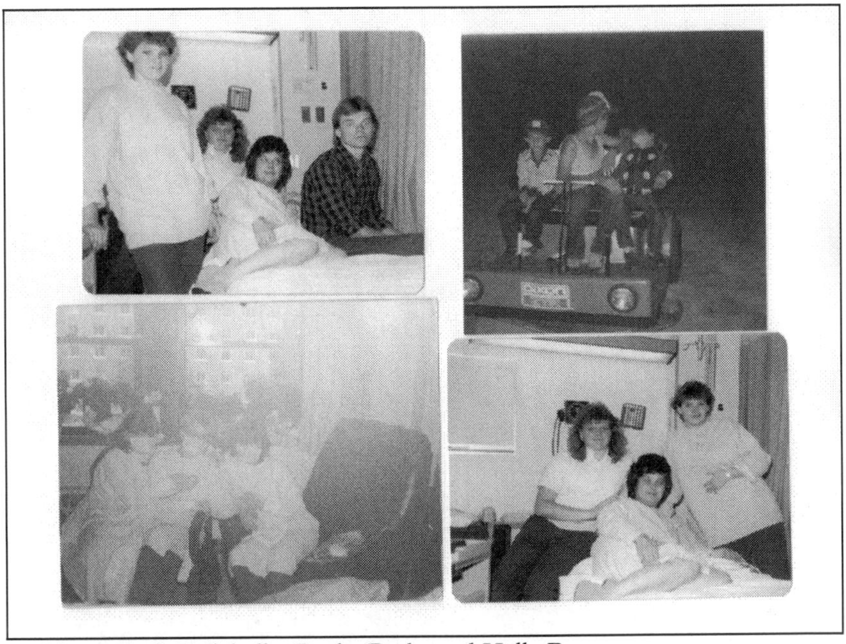

Upper Left: Michelle, Paula, Barb, and Kelly Pray.
Upper Right: Tigh Fliehs and friends.
Lower Left: Paula, Grandma Meta, and Michelle Pray.
Lower Right: Michelle, Barb and Michelle Pray

Alexa Rossman and Madeline Kelly, grandaughters.

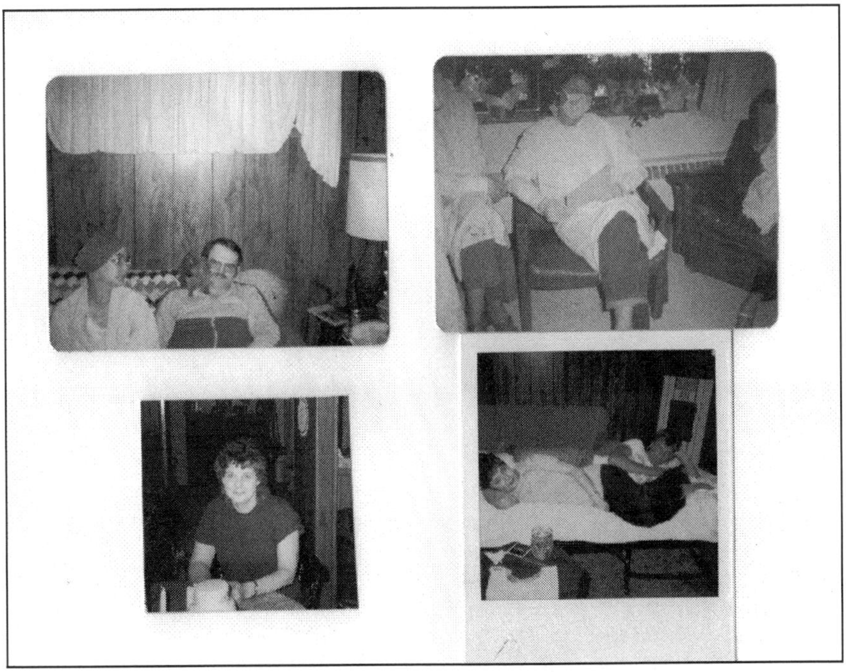

Left upper: Barb and Jim Pray
Right upper: Madonna Paulson.
Lower left: Barbara Pray.
Lower right: Barbara Pray and Kelly Pray.

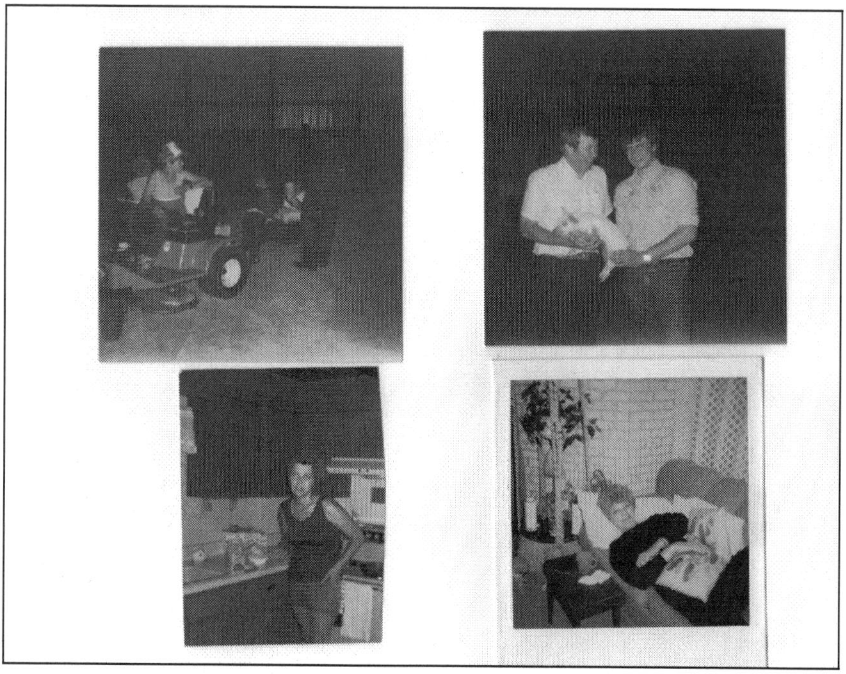

Upper left: Tigh Fliehs.
Upper right: Auctioneer,Steve Simon and Gary Fliehs held the benefit..
Lower left: Barb Pray, where the back had crumbled.
Lower right: Barb laying on the couch.

Tigh Fliehs and little piglet

Right upper: Barb Pray and Julie Hupke
Right lower: Barb Pray and Jim Pray.

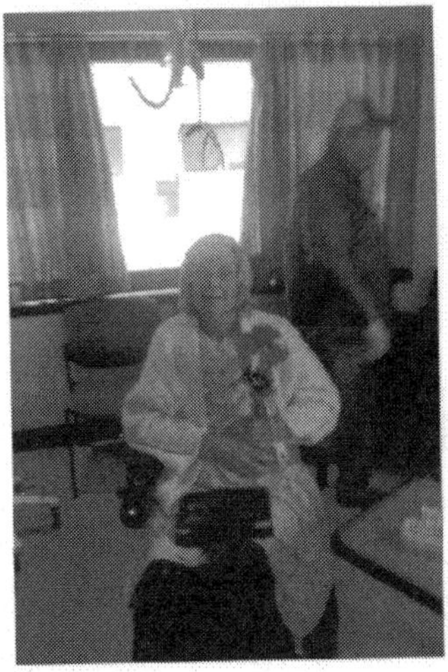

Barb and Jim Pray

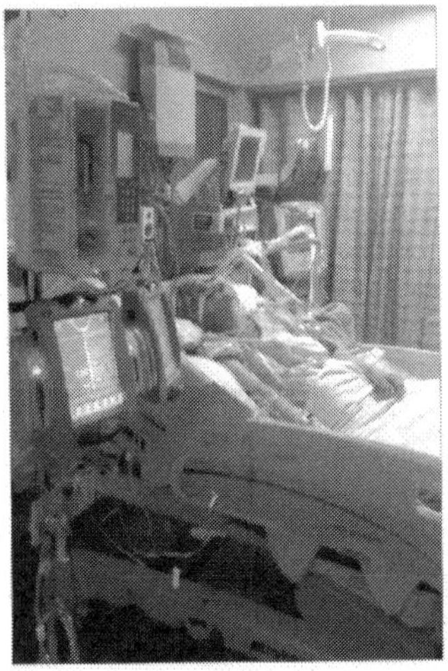

Barbara Pray

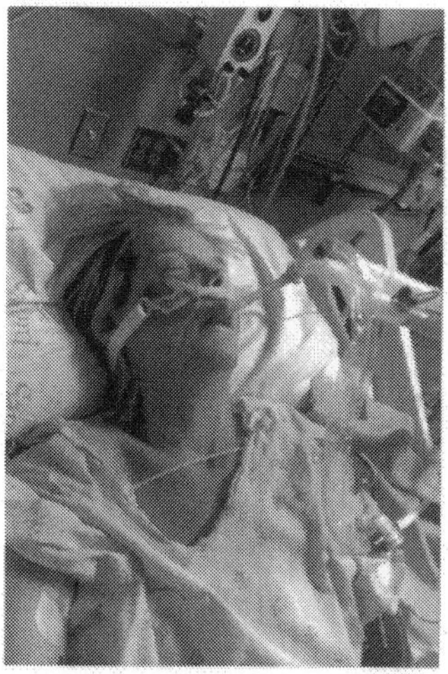

Display of Barb's photos. Barb in the hospital bed (2014).

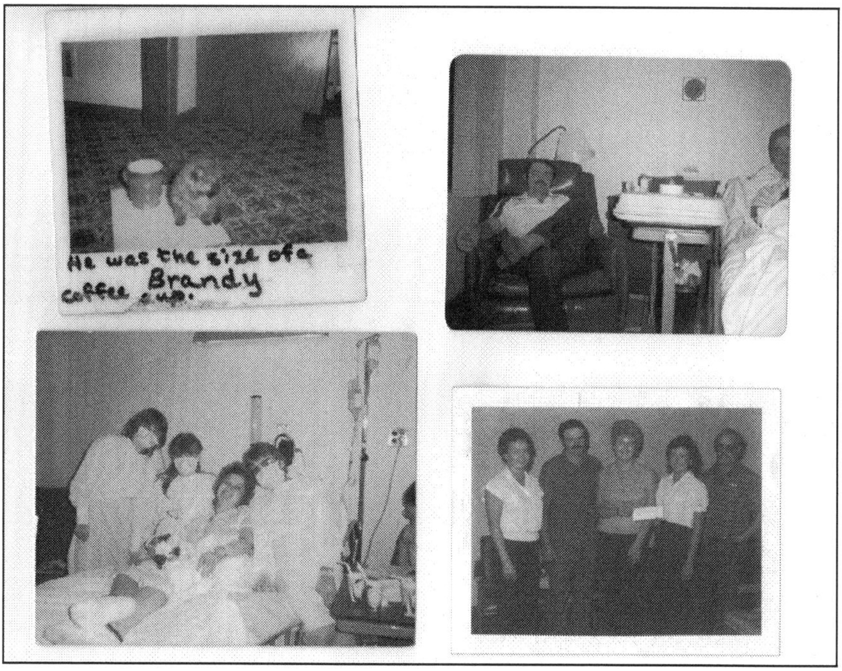


Upper left: Brandy, the miniature Pomeranian, the size of a coffee cup.
Upper right: Jim and Barb Pray.
Lower left: Michelle, Paula, Barb and Kelly Pray.1
Lower right: Rosemary Howard, Jim Pray, Barb Pray, Penny and Terry Anderson. The above presented to Jim and myself a check from the Groton City benefit.

Jim Pray and his combine.

Barb Pray and her family farm home.

Barb Pray.

Barb Pray.

Monday Morning Coffee Ladies
Upper Left to Right: Ruby Larson, Susan Kurth, Eunice McColister, Carol Osterman, Doris Tonwsend.
Lower Right to Left: Barb Pray, Linda Gengerke, JoAnn Krueger.
Not shown: Jackie Wagner and Gail Schinkel.

Shawn, Michelle, Madeline and Christopher Kelly.

Paula Pray's family

Paula Winther, Alexa Rossman and Paul Winther.

Kelly Pray's family

Kelly Pray, Christina and Kim Guerra.

Barb's Paper Tole picture that she crafted.

## Barb's Chicken Noodle Soup

Boil 1 whole chicken with 2-3 boxes of Swanson broth. Add to broth chopped carrots, chopped celery, chopped potatoes and chopped onion (optional). Barb doesn't use onion in her soup. Only chicken broth is used, no added water. Debone chicken and put small amount in soup. Save the rest of the chicken to put in the serving soup bowl. Salt and pepper to taste.

Noodles: Mix flour into 6 eggs, which have been whisked. Add enough flour to roll out in strips. The strips are then cut with a pizza cutter and put into boiling water and cooked until done. They will raise to the top when done. Watch them closely. Add to soup right before they are served.

33412060R00100

Made in the USA
Charleston, SC
13 September 2014